797,885 Books

are available to read at

www.ForgottenBooks.com

Forgotten Books' App
Available for mobile, tablet & eReader

ISBN 978-1-332-84018-2
PIBN 10179788

This book is a reproduction of an important historical work. Forgotten Books uses state-of-the-art technology to digitally reconstruct the work, preserving the original format whilst repairing imperfections present in the aged copy. In rare cases, an imperfection in the original, such as a blemish or missing page, may be replicated in our edition. We do, however, repair the vast majority of imperfections successfully; any imperfections that remain are intentionally left to preserve the state of such historical works.

Forgotten Books is a registered trademark of FB &c Ltd.
Copyright © 2015 FB &c Ltd.
FB &c Ltd, Dalton House, 60 Windsor Avenue, London, SW19 2RR.
Company number 08720141. Registered in England and Wales.

For support please visit www.forgottenbooks.com

1 MONTH OF
FREE
READING

at
www.ForgottenBooks.com

By purchasing this book you are eligible for one month membership to ForgottenBooks.com, giving you unlimited access to our entire collection of over 700,000 titles via our web site and mobile apps.

To claim your free month visit:

www.forgottenbooks.com/free179788

* Offer is valid for 45 days from date of purchase. Terms and conditions apply.

English
Français
Deutsche
Italiano
Español
Português

www.forgottenbooks.com

Mythology Photography **Fiction**
Fishing Christianity **Art** Cooking
Essays Buddhism Freemasonry
Medicine **Biology** Music **Ancient**
Egypt Evolution Carpentry Physics
Dance Geology **Mathematics** Fitness
Shakespeare **Folklore** Yoga Marketing
Confidence Immortality Biographies
Poetry **Psychology** Witchcraft
Electronics Chemistry History **Law**
Accounting **Philosophy** Anthropology
Alchemy Drama Quantum Mechanics
Atheism Sexual Health **Ancient History**
Entrepreneurship Languages Sport
Paleontology Needlework Islam
Metaphysics Investment Archaeology
Parenting Statistics Criminology
Motivational

THE

POEMS

OF

JOHN RUSKIN:

NOW FIRST COLLECTED FROM ORIGINAL MANUSCRIPT AND PRINTED
SOURCES; AND EDITED, IN CHRONOLOGICAL ORDER, WITH
NOTES, BIOGRAPHICAL AND CRITICAL,

BY

W. G. COLLINGWOOD.

VOLUME I.

POEMS WRITTEN IN BOYHOOD;

1826—1835.

GEORGE ALLEN,

SUNNYSIDE, ORPINGTON.

AND

8, BELL YARD, TEMPLE BAR, LONDON.

1891.

[All rights reserved.]

A 1
1891 b
v. 1

EDITOR'S INTRODUCTION.

FIRST POEMS; 1826, AGE 7.

This book is copyrighted in America by CHARLES E. MERRILL & CO., *New York* (1891).

become our own by sympathy : and when they reach the day of victory and coronation, we seem, like loyal adherents of a conqueror, to share the triumph ; and, like intimate confidants, to understand the full significance of the achievement.

It is no idle curiosity, then, that prompts the admirers of Mr. Ruskin's works to collect his boyish writings and to learn the story of his youth. More than other writers, he is misunderstood by the casual reader : more than

[All rights reserved.]

FIRST POEMS; 1826, AGE 7.

THERE is always a peculiar interest in watching development, in witnessing growth. When we have seen a plant burst the soil, and its long-expected bud unfold into blossom, we love every leaf and petal of it: it is our own; and worth more to us than all the cut bouquets of a flower-show. And in the same way we delight in the early history of nations,—in the early biography of great men. As we follow their first steps, and note the foreshadowings of character, the promises of power, which even their youngest years afford, they become our own by sympathy: and when they reach the day of victory and coronation, we seem, like loyal adherents of a conqueror, to share the triumph; and, like intimate confidants, to understand the full significance of the achievement.

It is no idle curiosity, then, that prompts the admirers of Mr. Ruskin's works to collect his boyish writings and to learn the story of his youth. More than other writers, he is misunderstood by the casual reader: more than

others, he needs to be approached—I do not say with
any prejudice in his favour—but with a preliminary
understanding of his ways, and aims, and attitude : and
in his case, more than with others, these conditions
have been determined at an early age, and illustrated
in his early writings.   That is the recurrent burden of
his autobiography :—"I find in myself nothing what-
soever *changed*.   Some of me is dead, more of me is
stronger.   I have learned a few things, forgotten many ;
in the total of me, I am but the same youth, disappointed
and rheumatic."

These poems, although he thrust them aside for prose,
in which he could better put the complicated feelings,
thoughts, and facts which he had to tell,—these poems
are, for that very reason, the best introduction to his
later and greater books.   They sketch the author's
portrait, as frontispiece to his works.   They give, in
the simple and direct terms to which lyrical or elegiac
verse is limited, the ground-plan of his character,—the
bias of his mental development.   They bring before
us, from year to year, his home and surroundings, his
studies and travels,—authentic memoirs of a curiously
observant childhood, in themselves valuable as records
of bygone times and old-world personages.   They
hint the models upon which he formed his style : and
the reader who is not tied down to admire whatever
affectation may be fashionable, of formality or of ex-
travagance, will find among these hitherto unknown

pieces much that will surprise him by its literary value.
I count it for nothing against them that their author
himself has never brought them forward : because he
has spent his best strength in elevating the public taste
in poetry as well as in art ; so that it was impossible for
him to offer his own juvenile productions as examples of
the lofty ideal he preached. But that makes me all the
more grateful to him for yielding to the requests of his
friends, and permitting the present publication.

Of Mr. Ruskin's earliest attempts at writing verse
he has given the following account :—"My calf-milk
of books was, on the lighter side, composed of Dame
Wiggins of Lee, the Peacock at Home, and the like
nursery rhymes ; and on the graver side, of Miss Edge-
worth's Frank, and Harry and Lucy, combined with
Joyce's Scientific Dialogues. The earliest dated efforts
I can find, indicating incipient action of brain-molecules,
are six 'poems' on subjects selected from those works ;
between the fourth or fifth of which my mother has
written : 'January, 1826. This book begun about
September or October, 1826 ; finished about January
1827.' The whole of it, therefore, was written and
printed in imitation of book-print in my seventh year ;"
that is, when he was seven years old. "Of the six
poems, the first is on the steam-engine, beginning

'When furious up from mines the water pours,
    And clears from rusty moisture all the ores ;'

and the last on the Rainbow, 'in blank verse,' as being
of a didactic character, with observations on the ignorant
and unreflective dispositions of certain people :

> ' But those that do not know about that light
>   Reflect not on it ; and in all that light
>   Not one of all the colours do they know.' " *

These are sufficient quotations from " The Steam-
engine " and " The Rainbow ; " but the same note-book
contains Mr. Ruskin's very first dated attempt at written
verse, composed in January 1826, before he had reached
the age of seven. As a curiosity, I print it just as he
copied it into that earliest edition of his poetical works,
—without punctuation, and with no capitals except in
the initial word, like a mediæval missal or an ancient
Greek codex :—

THE NEEDLESS ALARM.

AMONG the rushes lived a mouse
with a pretty little house
made of rushes tall and high
that to the skies were heard to sigh
while one night while she was sleeping
comes a dog that then was peeping
and had found her out in spite
of her good wall for then his sight
was better than our mouses
                       so
she was obliged to yield to foe

---

* Præterita, vol. i. chap. iii. (pp. 76, 83) ; and see the Editor's
account of the manuscripts of the unpublished poems, at the end of
this volume (p. 263).

when frightened was the dog just then
at the scratching of a hen
so of[f] he ran and little mouse
was left in safety with her house.

But these childish verses were not by any means merely derivative, as the author seems to hint in the passage quoted from *Præterita*.   His continuation of " Harry and Lucy," though it imitates Miss Edgeworth's form, is in great part the story of his own travels ; and two of the "poems" of this year, 1826, record the impressions received during a journey from Scotland with his parents, after visiting his aunt at Perth.   Of the " Farewell," line 4 is no doubt a reminiscence of the May sunshine in which they went northwards ; for their start was usually made about the middle of May ; and he contrasts the sunny anticipation of the arrival with the autumnal gloom of the departure.

FAREWELL TO SCOTLAND.

O what a change from pretty Perth so near,
To dreary heather, and to streams so clear,—
To rocks, and stones !   Upon the dreary way
No sun is shining, as on sprightly May.
Again it changes to the winding Earn,—
'Tis shallow water, but it has no fern ;
But it is precious for its shining drops ;
And sometimes from the river a fish pops.
Again it changes to a steep, steep hill,
And it is cold, do anything you will.

> In short, such changes Scotland does now take,
> That I can't tell them, and
>
> *an end I make*

was no doubt the conclusion he meant,—a not uncommon formula of termination in these first attempts, like the "these things were thus" with which Herodotus concludes his chapters. Note in passing, as a matter of style, the use of "precious" to describe the peculiar, unhackneyed beauty of a pet phenomenon.

During the journey home, or on his return, in September, was written a poem on "Glenfarg," which is extremely curious as a foretaste of that moralisation of landscape which is so characteristic of the author. It is interesting, also, from the precocious power of consecutive thought and condensed imagery, by which the little boy of seven rises in gradual climax from the river, in which he sees typified the mere "glory of going on and still to be" in the darkness of the ravine,—to the streams on the hillside, whose energy he fancies to be conscious of ministration to their fellow-creatures. From the streams, he ascends to the stones in them, which are called upon for a higher lesson,—to "bear" trial,—for he that endureth to the end shall "never, never die." But what in the stones is a virtue, is a defect in living creatures; for he sees the cattle live and move and have a fuller being; and the sheep still more so. And finally, man—proud of his earthly science, of the mill-wheel to which he trusts for his daily bread—is

reproved for the lowness of his horizon, and exhorted
to lift up his eyes to the wheel of the heavenly wain ;—
reminded of his fallible nature, and pointed to his true
guide and goal, above.

GLEN OF GLENFARG.

Glen of Glenfarg, thy beauteous rill,
 Streaming through thy mountains high,
Onward pressing, onward still,
 Hardly seeing the blue sky.

Mountain streams, press on your way,
 And run into the stream below ·
Never stop like idle clay,
 Hear the sheep, and cattle low.

Stones that in the stream do lie,
 Bear the rushing torrent still :
 Thou shalt never, never die,
 —Submit unto the Almighty's will.

Cows that lie upon the grass,
 Rise and graze upon the hills ;
Never be a heavy mass,
 Like a stone that's in the rills.

Sheep that eat upon the hills,
 Rise, and play, and jump about ;
Drink out of the running rills,
 And always on the grass be out.

Cottages upon the plain,
 Placed so near the floury mills ;
—Cottager, look on Charles's Wain,
 Right above the grassy hills.

The pole-star guides thee on the way,
When in dark nights thou art [lost];
Therefore look up at the starry day,
Look at the stars about thee tost.

The word in square brackets is wanting in the original. In the verses previously unedited, which nearly equal in bulk the already published poems, the few words that I have supplied or altered are marked in the same way, as also any notes or dates I have inserted: everything else in the body of the text is either given by Mr. Ruskin, or drawn from his writings, or from authorities immediately required for the sake of explanation. The Editor's notes are relegated to the end of the volumes. But while I have not taken liberties in the way of emending the original MSS., my instructions obliged me to omit such poems and passages as were either without general interest, or incomplete and inadequately representative of the author's attainments and style at the time; as must often be the case in verses written only in the rough, and never revised for publication. How completely unpolished the MSS. are may be gathered from the fact that they contain hardly a trace of punctuation. On the other hand, the spelling rarely needs correction.

The last piece of 1826 was a New Year's Address to the author's father, written apparently on December 31, as an essay to order; and, like other "commissions," without afflatus of inspiration. Shall I print it?—or

"discreetly blot"?   I think Mr. Ruskin's fame will
survive editorial indiscretion;—and "'tis sixty years
since," you know,—and more.   Besides, the "poem" is
meant to be humorous.

TIME.   BLANK VERSE.

Papa, what's Time?—a figure or a sense?
—'Tis one, but not the other.—Is not Time
A figure? yes, it is : for on the tops of shops
We often see a figure with two wings,
A scythe upon one shoulder, and a lock
Of hair upon his forehead, while his head is bald,
Except the lock upon his forehead ;—and called Time.
Time's very quick ; and therefore he has wings.
When past, Time's gone for ever ; so he has a lock
Of hair upon his forehead ; and the proverb is
"Take Time by the forelock."   He mows down every-
      thing,
And so he has a scythe.   Time is so quick
That might a year be called a day.
    Day !—Now I think of it, 'tis New Year's day.—
A happy New Year's day to you, Papa !
    And now I must return to Time.
Is Time only a figure? No, he is not.
What is he then ?—what is he ?—I don't know ;
He's not a quality ; of that I'm sure.
—Oh I remember now ! He is a god
Entitled Saturn : he's a heathen god.
And well he might be called one : none but they
Could go so quick, or jump from 'tween our hands
As Time does.   Time ! I'm quite away from him !
Away from him? No surely I'm not so ;
For I'm at heathen gods, and he's a god :
So though I may be from him, I'm not far
From him, and now I must go to him quite.

—'Tis but an hour to merry New-Year's day ;
For, though it is a day,—a day's an hour ;
And what's an hour,—'tis only a wee minute,
Made so by the quick course of time.
—So, Mr. Time, as I've said all about you,
All I've to say, I must take leave of you !

It is droll as it stands ; a very little touching up would
have regulated the rhythm and emphasised the grotesque
humour of the monologue.   The lad who, at the age of
seven, could knock this off without effort, and throw it
aside as a failure, was certainly taking time by the fore-
lock ;—father to the man who engraved upon his seal,
"To-day, To-day, To-day."   And is it not characteristic
that he should be already puzzling over the metaphysical
nature of Time, and, even though humorously, asking
questions that it took a Kant to answer?   Not long after,
he goes on to attempt an epic "On the Universe."
Surely this might have been Browning's youngster with
his "Transcendentalism ; a poem in twelve books : "
surely to this boy with "What a poetical face ! "—as
Keats' Severn said of him—might have been addressed
the admiring remonstrance, condensing all possible
criticism :—

"You are a poem, though your poem's naught.
The best of all you showed before, believe,
Was your own boy-face o'er the finer chords
Bent, following the cherub at the top
That points to God with his paired half-moon wings."

And to him surely, when the full time was come, the prophetic advice was appropriate, — how appropriate, with its Alpine metaphor !—

> "Speak prose, and hollo it till Europe hears !
> The six-foot Swiss tube, braced about with bark
> Which helps the hunter's voice from Alp to Alp—
> Exchange our harp for that,—who hinders you?"

But while recognising that Mr. Ruskin's power lay in other directions, it would be a mistake unduly to depreciate these volumes of juvenile verses. They contain many a sonorous line and noble thought, many a genuine feeling and fine, enthusiastic description that already

> "Buries us with a glory, young once more,
> Pouring heaven into this shut house of life."

CONTENTS.

---

* Pieces now Printed for the First Time.

1830; AGE 11.

1831; AGE 12.

1827

AT 8 YEARS OF AGE.

GLENFARG [*Autumn of* 1827].

THE SUN [*New Year's Address to his Father*, 1828].

VOL. 1.

GLENFARG.

I will risk whatever charge of folly may come on me, for printing one of my many childish rhymes, written on a frosty day in Glen Farg, just north of Loch Leven. . . . All that I ever could be, and all that I cannot be, the weak little rhyme already shows.

PAPA, how pretty those icicles are,
That are seen so near, that are seen so far;
—Those dropping waters that come from the rocks,
And many a hole, like the haunt of a fox;
That silvery stream that runs babbling along,
Making a murmuring, dancing song;
Those trees that stand waving upon the rock's side,
And men, that, like spectres, among them glide;
And waterfalls that are heard from far,
And come in sight when very near;
And the water-wheel that turns slowly round,
Grinding the corn that requires to be ground; *
And mountains at a distance seen,
And rivers winding through the plain;

* Political Economy of the Future!

3

And quarries with their craggy stones,
And the wind among them moans.*

* So foretelling Stones of Venice, and this essay on Athena.
Queen of the Air, iii. 12.) [On the date of this poem, see note i.
end of the volume.]

THE SUN.

[NEW YEAR'S ADDRESS TO HIS FATHER.]

THOU Sun, thou golden Sun, in beauty rise,
And show thy yellow face among the clouds;
Disperse the stars, and make bright morning come!
Break through the clouds, and let thy golden beams
Shine on the earth!   The birds, arising, sing
To hail the approach of thee.   At the hot noon
Oft have I worked to make my garden nice,
Till, when I stopped, the drops of perspiration
Fell from my brows.   In the sweet afternoon
The air is balmy; in that pleasant time
Oft have I walked, with dear Mamma beside me,
To watch the flowers growing, and to play
Upon the green.   Then comes the evening dark,
In which all nature quiet still remains.

When seven of these are past, a week is gone;
And four of these a month do constitute;
And twelve of these the long, long year do make.
But yet not all the year doth pass without
Some festivals; and some of these I'll name:—

First, solemn Easter comes ; then Whitsunday ;
Then Christmas,—New Year's Day.—
And New-Year's Day it is !   Therefore, Papa,
I must wish you a Happy New Year's Day !

[*Finished before January* 1, 1828.]

1828

AT THE AGE OF 9 YEARS.

MAY [*Birthday Address to his Father, May* 10, 1828].

SKIDDAW [*Summer of* 1828].

DERWENTWATER [*Summer of* 1828].

EUDOSIA ; ON THE UNIVERSE [*Spring and Autumn,* 1828].

MAY.

[BIRTHDAY ADDRESS TO HIS FATHER.]

FLOWERS spring up beneath thy feet;
Greenest velvet is thy seat;
  Sunny rays
  Round thee blaze,
With temperate and pleasant heat.
  Come away,
  Happy May,
Where all that's good and pleasant meet!

Much happier thou indeed to me,
For thou Papa's birthday doth see.
  With that thou might
  Be Zembla's night,
And yet be quite as fair to me
  As now thou art.
  My happy heart
Beats, at the thought of spending thee.

Not thee, May,—though indeed thou'rt fair,
'Tis for his birthday that I care;

That happy day
When joined with May
Is joyous more than all the year.
Come away,
Joyous May,
Good and happy, sweet and fair!

May 10.

SKIDDAW.

SKIDDAW, upon thy heights the sun shines bright,
But only for a moment: then gives place
Unto a playful cloud which on thy brow
Sports wantonly,—then floats away in air,—
Throwing its shadow on thy towering height;
And, darkening for a moment thy green side,
But adds unto its beauty, as it makes
The sun more bright when it again appears.
Thus in the morning on thy brow those clouds
Rest as upon a couch, and give vain scope
For fancy's play.   And airy fortresses,
And towers, and battlements, and all appear
Chasing the others off, and in their turn
Are chasèd by the others.
                           Skiddaw came,
Noble, and grand, and beauteous, clothed with green,
And yet but scantily and in some parts.
A bare, terrific cliff precipitous
Descends, with only here and there a root,
A straggler, pushing forth its branches stiff.
Skiddaw, majestic! Giant Nature's work!

Those giant works of Art,* with thee compared,
Sink into nothing; all that Art can do
Is nothing beside thee.   The touch of man
Raised pigmy mountains, but gigantic tombs.
The touch of Nature raised the mountain's brow,
But made no tombs at all; save where the snow
(The fleecy locks of winter) falls around
And forms a white tomb for the careless swain
Who wanders far from home, and meets his death
Amidst the cold of winter.

* [The Pyramids.]

[*Summer of* 1828.]

DERWENTWATER.

Now Derwentwater come !—a looking-glass
Wherein reflected are the mountain's heights,
As in a mirror, framed in rocks and woods ;
So upon thee there is a seeming mount,
A seeming tree, a seeming rivulet.
All upon thee are painted by a hand
Which not a critic can well criticise.
But to disturb thee oft, bluff Eolus
Descends upon the mountains, with his breath.
Thy polished surface is a boy at play
Who labours at the snow to make a man,
And when he's made it, knocks it down again ;—
As when thou'st made a picture thou dost play
At tearing it to pieces.   Trees do first
Tremble, as if a monstrous heart of oak
Were but an aspen leaf ; and then as if
It were a cobweb in the tempest's blow.
Thus like Penelope thou weav'st a web,
And then thou dost undo it.   Thou'rt like her
Because thou'rt fair, and oft deceiving too.

First seeming to be calm then turning rough,
And thus deceiving as Penelope.

Sweet Derwent, on thy winding shore,
Beside thy mountain-forests hoar,
There would I like to wander still,
And drink from out the rippling rill,
Which from thy mountain-head doth fall
And mingles with the eagles' call;
While on Helvellyn thunder roars,
Re-echoed from old Derwent's shores ;
And while the lightning flashes still,
Reflected in the mountain-rill.

[*Summer* 1828.]

EUDOSIA.

At nine years old I began a poem called Eudosia,—I forget wholly where I got hold of this name, or what I understood by it,— "On the Universe,"—though I could understand not a little by it, now. A couplet or two, as the real beginning at once of Deucalion and Proserpina, may be perhaps allowed a place in this grave memoir ; the rather that I am again enabled to give accurate date— September 28th, 1828,* for the beginning of its "First Book," as follows :—

WHEN first the wrath of heaven o'erwhelmed the world,
And o'er the rocks, and hills, and mountains, hurl'd
The waters' gathering mass, and sea o'er shore,—
Then mountains fell, and vales, unknown before,
Lay where they were. Far different was the Earth
When first the flood came down, than at its second
      birth.
Now for its produce !—Queen of flowers, O rose,
From whose fair coloured leaves such odour flows.
Thou must now be before thy subjects named,
Both for thy beauty and thy sweetness famed.
Thou art the flower of England, and the flow'r
Of Beauty too—of Venus' od'rous bower.

* [See note at end of volume.]

And thou wilt often shed sweet odours round,

And often stooping, hide thy head on ground.*

And then the lily, towering up so proud,

And raising its gay head amongst the various crowd.

There the black spots upon a scarlet ground,

And there the taper-pointed leaves are found.

In 220 lines, of such quality, the first book ascends from the rose to the oak. The second begins—to my surprise, and in extremely exceptional violation of my above-boasted custom—with an ecstatic apostrophe to what I had never seen ! (*Præterita*, Vol. I. chap. iii.)

EUDOSIA. Book II.

I sing the Pine, which clothes high Switzer's † head,

And high enthroned, grows on a rocky bed,

On gulphs so deep, on cliffs that are so high,

He that would dare to climb them dares to die.

There they hang o'er the dreadful rocky steeps,

There they bend over and they kiss the deeps,

Which round the rocks do play, and raging still

Awake the echoes from the waving hill.

But man this pleasing picture soon would spoil,

Regardless both of beauty and of toil,

Though nature tried in vain to save them for a while.

In vain to save them she did place them high :

Alas, in vain ! for they were doomed to die.

* An awkward way—chiefly for the rhyme's sake—of saying that roses are often too heavy for their stalks.

† Switzer, clearly short for Switzerland.

Man formed a slide,*—huge, pond'rous to behold;
It cost much labour and it cost much gold:
Along the breast of Pilate's cliff it lay,
O'er rocks, and gulfs, and glens, it held its way,
And ended in Lucerne. On this the trees,
Roaring like thundèr borne upon the breeze,
Rushed down; and rushing, dreadful in their ire,
To their assistance—such their anger dire—
Summoned with red and flaming crown that monster, Fire!
He then would have been King, and on the mount
The flaming forests would have spread about;
Another Etna Pilate would have been,—
O'er spacious Switzerland the fires be seen;
In one sad ruin all the pines would fall,—
In vain for help the noble forests call!

But man had this foreseen. Ingenious man
Thought, "Can I this prevent? Yes, if I will, I can!"
And so man made the mountain streams descend,
And down the trough their dang'rous course to bend:
This element opposed the raging fire,
And did prevent its great effects so dire.

Now comes the Hawthorn with its blossoms white,
Welcoming gaily in May's cheerful light.
With luscious odours it perfumes the breeze,
Most fair, most cheerful,—sweetest of the trees!

* "A description, verified out of 'Harry and Lucy,' of the slide of
Alpnach." (*Præterita*, I. iii.)

Bound up with clusters white, it doth adorn
The tall pole which is raised on May's first morn :
And, lightly bounding from the blooming green,
Round it the village youth are dancing seen.
Dandily dressed, with scarlet ribbons gay,
The sweeps with hawthorn welcome in the May;
With fluttering rags, with yellow and with red,
And hawthorn blossoms waving o'er their head.

And now the Yew, a mournful tree, I sing,
Which pois'nous is to every living thing.
And meet it is that such a tree is placed
In the dread churchyard, where the corses waste.
Now, think again !   In every case the yew
Shows death in all its terrors to the view.
For lo, see there !   Just bursting from the wood,
The free and lawless band of Robin Hood !
Look at their bows !   Tough yew confines the string,
And yew elastic gives the arrow wing,
Well aimed, and thirsting for the purple blood
Of tallest stag that ever ranged the wood.
The wingèd dart flies gladly through the air,
And quickly fixes in its body fair.
The tall stag fainteth with the deadly wound,
And, deeply sighing, sinks upon the ground.

And now, dost see yon ruined pile on high,
Majestic, creeping up against the sky?

Behold the Ivy creeping o'er the stone,
Which still remains from luxury that's gone.
Where now foul weeds arise, and tempests sweep
O'er the vast hall and tower and donjon-keep,
In former times were feasts, and blazing fires,
And mirth, and everything the soul desires.
Time hath flown by with mouldering touch ;—hath past,
And mirth and luxury have breathed their last.

1829.

AT THE AGE OF 10 YEARS.

THE YELLOW FOG [*March*].

THE MOON (*June* 28).

ON HAPPINESS (*July* 19).

SABBATH MORNING (*Aug.* 2–16).

SHAGRAM'S FAREWELL TO SHETLAND (*Oct.* 18).

ETNA (*Oct.* 25).

my dear papa

A good Newyear to you I at
intended to make for your Newyears present a
model of any easily done thing and I thought I
try to make an orrery but at length I gave it up
considering how many different things were wanted and
used the inclosed poem with another short address to
but Mamma disliking my address and telling me to
a small letter to you I attempted though I will
say I have succeeded to do it which thing I hope you
accept however unworthy it be of your
dear papa
your affectionate son
John Ruskin

Hernhill
December thirty first 1828

But frightened was the preacher when
He heard all echoed down the glen
The music of the clans
Twas martial music and around
5 Well echoed was the beauteous sound
By valley rock and hill
It died away upon the ear
And spread abroad now there now here
And gathered strength again
10 And now the flute and now the drum
Mingling upon the winds they come
And die away again
Another strain another sound
And now tis silence all around
15 The martial music's gone.

ON THE APPEARANCE OF A SUDDEN CLOUD OF YELLOW FOG COVERING EVERYTHING WITH DARKNESS.

IT low'red upon the earth,—it lay
A champion in the face of day:
It darkened all the air around,
It let not free a single sound
A leaf stirred not: the trees stood still;
The wind obeyed the darkness' will;
Not a thing moved; 'twas like the night.
The darkness faced the warrior, Light;
They fought; the darkness conquered; still
Light obeyed not the conqueror's will,
But yet kept up a twilight day,
Though he below the darkness lay.
And now big drops of rain fell round,
And soon unloosed the chains of sound.
Again they fought; new light arose,
And joined to fight with darkness' foes.
Darkness fought well, but could not stand;
He cried " I want a helping hand."
He sunk; and then he cried " I yield,

I yield this well-contested field."
And now the birds began to sing
Because now sound became a king;
And now the twilight went away,—
At length arose the wished-for day.

[*March.*]

THE MOON.

FAIR Luna, shining on thy cloudy car,
Riding in state, on spangled heaven afar,
Where, when the sun hath sunk upon the hill,
Thou dost dispense his light upon us still ;—
Now, tipped with silver, messenger of night,
A dark, black cloud o'erhangs thy silver light,
Now half-obscured ; but now thy light once more
Doth tip with silver every mountain hoar,
Shines on the vale, and on the ocean's breast
With glittering glory doth the waves invest.
And, as the waves roll on to gain the shore,
Their white foam, silvered, glitters more and more.
A tide of glory spreads along the waves ;
Their moving breasts the flood of brightness laves.
But when, at last, the sun, from whom the light
Of the fair moon doth interrupt the night,
Rises once more upon that eastern gold,
The pale moon's story to the earth is told ;
And with her glittering diamonds from the skies
That beauteous orb of night with her attendants flies.

June 28.

ON HAPPINESS.

O WHAT is Happiness? that precious thing
Rare, and in great request; yet seldom found:
Sought for in various ways in which it seems
To be within the reach. Now try! Behold
Active, it yet eludes the searcher's grasp
And leads him, hopeful, on; then disappoints him;
And now at last he tries the paths of vice.
Happiness is not there. In vain with drink
He tries to gain a transient gleam of joy.
But soon he sinks again; and plunged in grief
He feels the stings of conscience; and he ends
With launching out into eternity,
While his own hands do push the boat from shore.

July 19.

SABBATH MORNING.

SEE where the sun doth on that hill arise,
    And look where Phœbus snatches up the reins :
See where his radiance paints the morning skies,
    And where unwillingly the darkness wanes!

The dewdrops glitter to the rising sun,
    With diamonds decking all the trees so fair ;
Frail in their beauty, melting one by one,
    And in a vapour thickening all the air.

Above, in robe of blue adorned so fair,
    Speckled with small white clouds is that fair sky,
Which gently float upon the balmy air,
    Hiding the skylark as it warbles high.

Now, borne on waving air the church-bell rings,
    Pleasing the ear, as tolls it, softly slow ;
Sound following sound, full heavily it swings,
    And in sweet cadence rolls its music low.

August 2–16,

SHAGRAM'S FAREWELL TO SHETLAND.

1.

Farewell, my dear country, so savage and hoar!
I shall range on thy heath-covered Sumburgh no more;
For lo! I am snatched to a far distant shore,
  To wish for my country in vain.

2.

This green dancing sea that now bears me away,
I have seen it with pleasure on some stormy day
To dash 'gainst the cliffs, and throw up its white spray,
  Roaring, as tossed the high surge.

3.

Ah! little I thought that its bosom so fair
Me away from my country and wild heaths should bear;
For I hate the green fields and the warm southern air,
  When compared with my dear native home.

4.

They say it is savage, and covered with snow;
But still purple heather and grass are below;
And I care not, though o'er it the cold breezes blow,
For still it is fertile to me!

5.

Wild roar the waves as they dash on the rocks;
And double and treble their thundering shocks;
And their foam still it rolls like a thousand white flocks,
With their fleeces all white as the snow.

6.

But I look for my country, and round me I gaze;
Yet nothing is seen, save the surge as it plays;
And those fair western clouds, still illumed by the rays
Of the sun, as it sinks 'neath the ocean.

7.

My dear native land! I have parted from thee;
And thy high hill of Rona no more I can see:
From this time, woe and sorrow are destined to me,
Though I'm borne unto Albion's shore.

18th October.

ETNA.

On old Sicilia's isle a mountain roars
In sounds re-echoed from Italia's shores.
Lo! in the sable night, when mankind sleep,
And when each creature rests in slumber deep,
Oft there is heard a rumbling, rolling sound,
Which back Messina's rocky straits rebound.
Such is the thunder, that the mountains quake,
And the huge earth itself is felt to shake.
At the dread moment, houses,—cities fall;
The earth gapes wide; destruction swallows all.

Then Etna from his burning crater pours
A fiery torrent o'er Sicilia's shores.
Down, down his side the lava-rivers flow,
And the hot streams o'erwhelm all, all below!
While, from the crater, gaseous vapours rise;
Volcanic lightnings flash along the skies;
Earth gapes again: Catania's city falls,
And all her people die within her walls.

And now at length the Etnæan lavas stay,
And cease to roll along upon their way.

Etna is quiet ; but it leaves a scene
That well may fill with fear the hearts of men.
O'er all Sicilia desolation reigns,
And by the lavas burnt are fruitful plains.
But on the buried cities others rise ;
And soon again green verdure meets the eyes.

25th October.

1830.

AT 11 YEARS OF AGE.

TRAFALGAR (*Feb.* 12).
MY DOG DASH (*April* 30).
HADDON HALL [*about June or July*].
ON THE DEATH OF MY COUSIN JESSIE (*Sept.* 9).
THE ASCENT OF SKIDDAW [*Nov.-Dec.*].

TRAFALGAR.

Upon the Atlantic's spacious breast
  The British ships come on;
Full many a soul shall go to rest,
  Ere the fatal day is done.
The waves rose dancing at the prow,
  In foaming, sparkling spray,
And each surge was tipped with a crest of snow
  As the warships cut their way.
And on the waves which tossed around
The murderous lines of cannon frowned.

Now, with a wild and hissing sweep,
A ball there dashes o'er the deep.
Then, flash on flash, and roar on roar,
The British ships began the war.

There, through the volumes of the smoke,
The lightning flash of cannon broke;
And the high-bounding, crested wave
Was tinged with the blood of the dying brave;
And darkness, rising drear and dread,
On the field of death her wings outspread.

Now the Spanish line gave way;
Now the British won the day.
But the Spanish parting volley gave
A naval hero to the grave.
Fearless on the stern he stood,
Looking on the purple flood.
One parting flash,—one bursting roar,—
Trafalgar's hero rose no more!

Then the British hearts beat high,
Then lightning flashed from every eye;
"Revenge!" burst wildly on the breeze,—
"Revenge!" it sounded o'er the seas.
With killing rage, with murderous roar
The British on the Spaniards bore.
Now, o'er the field of battle dread,
A sudden blaze there shone;
And every bloody billow bore
A brightness not its own:
As when the setting sun doth lave
Its glories in the ocean wave;
And when the gentle evening breeze
Curls the light ripple of the seas,
Which, glancing in the rays so bright,
Reflect a glittering line of light.
So, blazing high, sublime and dread
The flames rose flashing overhead.
When, sudden, to the skies arose
A far re-echoing sound

And broken masts, and splintered boards,
    And flames were tossed around :
And sinking in the ocean deep
The brave together calmly sleep.

And now the Spanish foemen fled
Full swiftly o'er the Atlantic main ;
And, while lamenting for their dead,
They sought the Spanish land again.
Meantime, the mourning victors bore
Their Nelson to his native shore ;
And a whole weeping nation gave
Funereal honours to the brave.
Where was the eye that did not give
    One single, bitter tear?
Where was the man that did not weep
    Upon Lord Nelson's bier?

February 12.

MY DOG DASH.

I HAVE a dog of Blenheim birth,
With fine long ears, and full of mirth;
And sometimes, running o'er the plain,
   He tumbles on his nose:
But, quickly jumping up again,
   Like lightning on he goes!
'Tis queer to watch his gambols gay;
He's very loving—in his way
He even wants to lick your face,
But that is somewhat out of place.
'Tis well enough your hand to kiss;
But Dash is not content with this!
Howe'er, let all his faults be past,
I'll praise him to the very last.

30th April.

HADDON HALL.

"To my farther great benefit, as I grew older, I thus saw nearly all the noblemen's houses in England; in reverent and healthy delight of uncovetous admiration. . . . And to this day, though I have kind invitations enough to visit America, I could not, even for a couple of months, live in a country so miserable as to possess no castles." (*Præterita*, I. i.)

I.

Old halls, and old walls,—
  They are my great delight;
Rusty swords, and rotten boards,
  And ivy black as night!
Hey, ruination and hey, desolation,—
Only created to spoil the creation!

II.

Dry ditch, old niche,—
  Besides, an oaken table;
On't the warriors ate,
From a .pewter plate,
  As much as they were able!
Hey, ruination and hey, desolation,—
Only created to spoil the creation!

[*About June or July*].

ON THE DEATH OF MY COUSIN JESSIE.

. . . "My little cousin Jessie, then traversing a bright space between her sixth and ninth year; dark-eyed deeply, like her mother, and similarly pious; so that she and I used to compete in the Sunday evening scriptural examinations; and be as proud as two little peacocks because Jessie's elder brothers, and sister Mary, used to get 'put down,' and either Jessie or I was always 'Dux.' We agreed upon this that we would be married when we were a little older; not considering it to be preparatorily necessary to be in any degree wiser. . . .

"Not long after that, when we were back at home, my cousin Jessie fell ill, and died very slowly, of water on the brain." (*Prae-terita*, I. iii.-iv.)

OH, ye restless deeps, that continually roll on your everlasting waves, swell the moaning of your waves, and the harmony of your billows, to a dirge for her who is departed!

For, colder than the foam, which, not so pure as her spirit, is rising on the crest of your billows, she reposes in the grave.

O ye winds of heaven, breathe in melancholy notes a song of death!

Youth is departed; beauty is withered in the grave.

She, whose step was lighter than the roe's, and whose eye was brighter than the eagle's,—her dust is consigned to the dust : she is gone to a home from which she shall not return ; to a rest which is eternal, to a peace which is unbroken.

She is freed from her sufferings ; she is released from her pains.

Why should I mourn for her who is departed? · *She* is not consigned to the dust,—*she* is not given to the grave !

She is not a prey to the worms, and her beauty is not departed !

Her soul is ethereal ; her spirit is with its God. She is fairer and purer than on earth.

Why should I mourn for the spirit which is returned to its Maker?

I will not mourn ; I will rejoice for her who is praising her Creator,—who is joining in the harmony of heaven.

9th September.

THE ASCENT OF SKIDDAW.

[THE START.]

THE hills were obscured in a curtain of cloud;
Every stern, savage fell had its vapoury shroud.
As we looked on the clouds with great feelings of sorrow,
How sadly we thought, "We must wait till to-morrow!"
Sometimes we did mope, as the clouds passed us by;
And again we did hope, as appeared the blue sky.
At length into distance the vapours were borne,
And the dreary gloom yields to the rays of the morn:
On the breast of the breeze were the clouds borne away,
And the mountains again were revealed to the day.
We gazed on the sky, now so azure and bright,—
We gazed on the sky with unmingled delight.
How high beat our hearts with the great expectation!
And straight we began to make great preparation.
Cakes, sandwiches, ham, were by no means unhandy;
And amongst other things we forgot not some brandy.
We stretch and we yawn, so impatient to go,
And think that the time flies amazingly slow!
We pull out our watch; put it up to our ear;
"Ah well, I declare, it is going, I hear!"

Then in comes the hostess, so prim and so neat,—

" A very fine morning, sir ! "—" 'Tis, ma'am, indeed."

" I have brought, sir, some skirts for the ladies to ride
in ; "

" Oh, ma'am, I declare your extremely obligin' ! "

" Oh, sir, pray don't speak of it ! "   While saying so,

She maketh her exit, in curtseying low.

And now a loud clatter is heard in the yard,

Where the steeds for the journey at length were prepared.

Oh, what an affair of importance then made is,

While settling and helping and mounting the ladies !

" I am sure I shall fall !   I am sure I am tumbling ! "—

" Oh, no, ma'am, you're safe."—" But my steed is a-
stumbling ! "

" Oh, ma'am, he's the surefooted'st beast upon earth ! "

" My saddle is loose ! "—" Shall I tighten the girth ? "

" Oh, but look at him now ; he is stopping and feeding."

" Pull him up, ma'am ! "—" I can't ! "—" Then I see I
must lead him."

Such pranks and such frolics our chargers displayed,

And such a great bustle and rumpus is made :

While laughing and talking swift onwards we trot,

And all ills and all accidents soon are forgot.

But some troubles still the ascending attended,

For the road, I must say, wanted much to be mended :

The quagmires were long, and the quagmires were broad,

And many and deep were the ruts of the road.

And while in the regions of heat we remained,

Of the heat and the flies we all loudly complained.

But we cared not for mud and we cared not for mire,
For our bosoms beat high with a lofty desire;
When the summit of Skiddaw was once in our view,
Through all opposition resistless we flew!
Till, having arrived at the breast of the hill,
To rest and to breathe, we a moment stood still.

[THE VIEW FROM LATRIGG.]

The vapourless heaven shone bright overhead,
The valley beneath us was widely outspread;
And the forests, arrayed in their clothing of green,
On the sides of the mountains arising were seen:
While, through the wide valley meandering slow,
The stream of the Derwent doth silently flow.
We gazed on the lake,—oh, how calmly it lay,
Scarce touched by the zephyrs o'er 'ts bosom which
        play!
How bright its smooth surface deceitfully smiles,
Embosomed in mountains, and studded with isles,
Whose trees, richly clothed in a bright living green,
Again seemed to grow 'neath the surface serene.
Then we gazed down the lake, where swift rushed to the
        shore
The far-sounding waters of distant Lodore;
As, hurled down the chasm, how thundering it broke,
Rebounding from crag, and rebounding from rock!
Then we looked to the south, where the dark Borrowdale
Frowned drear o'er the Derwent, stern, savage and fell;

While under those cliffs e'en the surges that sweep
Seemed mournfully silent, dark, dismal and deep.
While hidden in mist, and obscurèd by storm,
Gaunt Castle-Crag rose; oh, how dreadful its form!
And it guarded those Jaws which seemed deep as the
     grave,
As they frowned o'er the foam of broad Derwent's light
     wave.

[THE CLIMB.]

Thus the beautiful prospect we all did survey;
Then began to prepare for the rest of the way:
Some sandwiches take, and some brandy we sip,
Applying it just to the tip of the lip.
And our spirits revived, and restorèd our strength,
We set off on the rest of our journey at length.
How jollily onwards we all of us went!
But our eyes to the ground we were forced to keep
     bent,
For fear that our steeds in their progress should stumble,
And that might produce a most unlucky tumble.
Avoiding each hillock, each stone and each stick,
The steps of our ponies we carefully pick.
And still we ascended, still higher and higher,
And still to the summit came nigher and nigher.
And still we kept laughing and talking, and still
We trotted along at the side of the hill,
Till we reached an ascent where low hillocks of green,
Like mountainous molehills, were everywhere seen.

We dashed on our steeds and we spurred up the
     rise ;—
Oh sight most delightful that greeted our eyes !
A ridge we beheld ('twas of loose slaty stone) ;
It led to the summit we'd wished for so long.
But now our teeth chattered, our noses looked blue
And our ears were assuming a ruby-like hue.
Then to guard 'gainst the cold we did button our coats,
Protecting our bodies with mantles and cloaks ;
Then tight round our necks we did tie our cravats,
More firm to our heads we did fasten our hats
Then, steady and ready, we made up our mind
To fight and to conquer the cold and the wind.
So struggling we forced o'er the ridge of loose stone,—
Every second we thought we should over be blown ;
And although of its force we did loudly complain,
The summit of Skiddaw at last we attain.

[THE SUMMIT.]

How frowned the dark rocks which, bare, savage and
     wild,
In heaps upon heaps were tremendously piled !
And how vast the ravines which, so craggy and deep,
Down dreadful descending divided the steep !
Stay ! hark to the eagle ! how shrill is its cry,
From the breast of the hill which re-echoes on high !
Then, borne on the breezes which softly do play,
Tow'rd the fells of the Derwent it dieth away.

Again from these rocks it doth suddenly break,
And sounding as shrilly, it sweeps o'er the lake ;
Then echoed again from gigantic Grassmoor,
And sharply rebounding from shore unto shore.
But where is the mountain-bird ? Where doth he spring ?
Where beats the breeze backward the flap of his wing ?
Lo, see where, impelled by his tempest-like force,
In cloud-hidden circles he wheels on his course ;
O'er the rock-beating torrent he fearless is soaring ;
Scarce hearing its thunders eternally roaring !
Then turned we around to the maze of the mountains,
All teeming and sparkling with thousand bright fountains :
Where the brow of Helvellyn superior towered,—
Where the beetling Sca-Fell so tremendously lowered,—
Tost confusedly in clusters all barren and grim,
While the clouds o'er their sky-braving battlements
        skim ;
Till, their scarce-discerned outlines all misty and grey,
On the distant horizon they faded away.

[HAEC OLIM MEMINISSE.]

Now tell me, oh reader, hast tasted repose
When toilings and labours have come to a close ?
Hast thou gloried when thou hast successfully toiled
In overcome dangers and diff'culties foiled ?
Oh, then and then only thou fitly canst tell
How our hearts lightly beat and our proud bosoms
        swell.

Delighted we sat round the bright blazing fire,
And talked of our hardships,—the mountain, the
Though other things sink in the chaos of thought,
And fly from our mem'ry, let all be forgot,
As light chaff is borne on the face of the wind,
Yet Skiddaw shall ne'er be erased from our mind.

[*Nov.-Dec.*]

[*PASSAGES FROM*] *THE ITERIAD; OR, THREE WEEKS AMONG THE LAKES.*

[*From Kendal to Low-wood; Sunset at Low-wood; Grasmere; Helvellyn; Thirlmere; Keswick.*
January-March.

Friar's Crag and Castlehead; Hero-worship; Borrowdale in a Shower; Honistar Crag; Thunderstorm at Buttermere.
March–May.

Mythological Meteorology; Ullswater, a digression; Coming down from Kirkstone; Excursion to Coniston.
July–September].

TO MY HEART (*Jan.* 26).

TO POESIE (*March* 11).

WANT OF A SUBJECT [*about March*].

TO THE OCEAN-SPIRITS (*June* 20).

TO THE FAIRIES (*June* 20).

BEDTIME [*about September*].

TO THE MEMORY OF SIR WALTER SCOTT (*October*).

THE ETERNAL HILLS [*about October*].

THE SITE OF BABYLON (*Nov.* 6).

MOONLIGHT ON THE MOUNTAINS (*Nov.* 30).

SONNET. HARLECH CASTLE [*end of* 1831].

SONNET TO A CLOUD [*end of* 1831].

[PASSAGES FROM]

THE ITERIAD;

OR, *THREE WEEKS AMONG THE LAKES.*

[FROM KENDAL TO LOW-WOOD.]

As, eagerly waiting the dawn of the day
And sleeplessly counting the moments, I lay,
I thought of the joys that my bosom should know,—
Of the rich tides of pleasure unmingled which flow;
Unmingled with grief, and unmingled with gall,
But draughts of delight,—rapture,—banquetings all!
At length the time came, when, the bill being made,—
Boots, hostler and chambermaid all duly paid,—
Sticks, bonnets, hats, great-coats, all duly prepared;—
Our 'elegant carriage' rolled out of the yard!
Oh, the rapturous vision! But cease this vain rhyme
Which, not at all needed, wastes paper and time,—
Too lengthened and tiresome. Sufficient to say
That we entered our carriage, and rattled away.

Oh, thrice happy moment, when Windermere's sheet
In its bright, silvan beauty lay stretched at our feet!

With uplifted hands, and with praise never-ending,
The hill we were slowly, most slowly, descending;
And, feasting our eyes on the prospect before,
With lingering steps we were nearing the shore
Until we were plunged, as we turned to the right,
In a wood that obscured the scene from our sight;
Save when some opening space for a moment revealed
The scene, scarce perceived when again 'twas concealed.

I much love to gaze on a ven'rable wood,
Which for ages and centuries past may have stood,—
Upon oaks, with their mossy trunks gnarlèd and knotted,
Which still are majestic, decayed though and rotted;
With their far-spreading branches, obscuring the day
From the green, wooded glades and the birches so grey.
So fair was the wood on which now we did gaze,
Admiring the flowery, moss-carpeted maze:
And there, a small streamlet with verdant banks sung
As it laughingly sported the green-sward among.

And now, as we gladly emerged from the shade,
The place of our halting at length we surveyed.
We drove to the door, and the bell it was rung,
And forth from the carriage impatient we sprung.
Our apartment was shown,—to the window we flew,—
But oh, what a prospect awaited our view!

We saw on the opposite side of the road
That four lofty poplars 'sky-scrapingly' stood;

While, festooning and twining their foliage among,
The ivy so gracefully garlanded clung.
They stood on a bank which the crystalline wave
Of the wood-skirted Windermere lightly did lave,—
So fresh, and so cooling, as angry it broke
On a pier that was formed of rough masses of rock.
Two barks the waves breasted, but moored by a chain
In vain that wave bore them, they struggled in vain.
Then wandered the eye, as deserting the shore
It roved the dark lake and its blue mountains o'er ;
Where the huge pikes of Langdale struck awe to the
        mind,
With their dark and dread outlines distinctly defined ;
Where the pikes of Sca-fell rose so haughty and proud
While its battlements lofty looked down on the cloud,—
While its sides with ravines and dark chasms were riven,—
That huge mountain-wall seemed upholding the heaven !

[SUNSET AT LOW-WOOD.]

THE sun, ere his glory away should be past,
On the brows of the mountains was shining his last.
The bright western clouds their rough outlines unfold,
Relieving their splendour and graven in gold.
Methought little space 'tween those hills intervened,
But nearer,—more lofty,—more shaggy they seemed.
The clouds o'er their summits they calmly did rest,
And hung on the aether's invisible breast ;

Than the vapours of earth they seemed purer, more
    bright,—
Oh! could they be clouds? 'Twas the necklace of night!
Then we looked on the lake, where the deep crimson
    ray
Shot its light on the waters, as bloody they play;
It seemed as if autumn had given its tinge
To the woods, which the lake's splendid ripples did
    fringe
And the islands, on which that bright rippling rolled,
They seemed as if lashed by the pure liquid gold.
Oh! such was the scene which in glory reposed;—
But soon by the evening its splendour was closed:
Ere we reached our home, the dark shades of the night,
Descending, had hidden the hills from our sight;
They died in the mists of the darkness away,
To be waked into light at the dawn of the day.

[GRASMERE.]

AND now towards the green banks of Grasmere we prest,
Where it stretched 'mid the valley its hill-shaded breast.
And now,—as ere evening concluded the day
Our journey o'er many a wild mountain lay,—
At the inn which is built on the banks of the lake
We determined our dinner or luncheon to take.
But, in order that we to the inn might attain,
We were forced to turn down by a long, narrow lane.

But it twisted and turned so, to left and to right,
With its hedges obscuring the inn from our sight,
That we, all its troublesome windings not knowing,
Were all the time wondering where we were going !
And fears which were quite of a different kind
Were intruding and pushing themselves on our mind.
Suppose, in our way that a carriage should come,—
The road was so narrow !—what then should be done ?
Then 'twas certain and sure that one of us must back.
Back ?—back !—why we *might* have backed into the lake !
What should we say then to Miss Fortune so fickle ?
Then truly she'd have put us into a pickle !
But these accidents only existed in thought,
For safely and soon to the inn we were brought.

And now an excursion we thought we would make,
A view of the lake and the valley to take ;
So, enquiring the way to a small elevation,
Whose summit we thought a most excellent station,
First, we gazed where Helm-crag to the west of the vale
Reared its cloud-splitting head, and lower'd down on the
          dale.
But the terrified eye, now deserting its form—
The abode of the tempest, the pris'n of the storm—
To the fields of the valley beneath it would rove,
Which seemed sacred to peace, and to heaven-born
          love ;
Where the husbandman's labours repaid him tenfold,
All rich in their wavings and growing in gold ;

And their grain-loaded heads as they bent in the breeze
Seemed soft, rolling waters and billowy seas.
And the cattle, they mingle their soft-sounding lowing
With the sound of the streams through the fields that are
        flowing;
Till the valley was checked by the opposite hills
All dotted with sheep and all sparkling with rills:
While far to the south, the lake spreads its fair waves,
And the meadows which stoop to its edges it laves.

And now, when the prospect we all had surveyed,
A descent we remembered at last must be made.
But wherever our steps we were carefully bending
Oh! still that moss-path was as steep in descending,—
So, half rolling, half going,—half tumbling, half walk-
        ing,—
Half laughing, half giggling,—half tittering, half talking;—
Now surveying a streamlet, now mineralizing,—
Now admiring the mountains, and now botanizing,—
We came to the inn; and set off when we'd dined,
And ascending a hill, we left Grasmere behind.

[HELVELLYN.]

First, the giant Helvellyn arose on the right,—
Helvellyn, Helvellyn,—that mountain of might!
Peaked rocks, over dark, gloomy gorges impending,—
And a torrent down every ravine was descending.

Cloud-born, o'er the precipice stern they did break,
And, tumultuously foaming, were lost in the lake;
Appearing, as brightly they dashed from on high,
Like threads of pure silver which hung from the sky.
Midway on the face of the cliff the clouds rode;
High above rose the mountain, the eagle's abode.

[THIRLMERE.]

So distinctly reflected the margin so green,
The wave seemed unbounded—its border, unseen:
And, half-overhanging the silent, blue tide,
The opposite hills stretched their heath-covered side.
How bright,—how luxuriant, looked the thick heath,
Its rich purple bells as 'twas bending beneath,
Its patches rich shaded with fern as it grew,
And mantled the hill with its Tyrian hue.
While, beyond, a dark chaos of mountains was tost,
And hills after hills in the distance were lost ·
While the sun, ere he dies on the mountains away,
Was shedding his brightest,—but transient—ray.
Now reaching our carriage, with lingering look,
Of Helvellyn and Thirlmere our farewell we took;
By rock and by brooklet swift galloping on,
And holding our course by the Vale of St. John,
As the sun was just setting, and late was the time,
We hastened tall Castlerig's windings to climb.

[KESWICK.]

AND now we arrived at the brow of the hill,
Where the vast dale of Keswick lay sweetly and still.
To the right, on the north of the valley, we saw
The majestical form of the lofty Skiddaw.
In a proud amphitheatre,—mountainous,—dread,
Below us fair Derwent in glory was spread.
On rocky isles covered with verdure, and bays,
On capes jutting out, and on forests we gaze,
Which relieved the dark mountains in distance and gloom,
And chasms as deep and as drear as the tomb.
Now on rugged Grasmoor the red sun dies away,
And evening comes down with her mantle of grey.

[FRIAR'S CRAG AND CASTLEHEAD.]

WHEN breakfast was done on the following day,
As impatient we were Derwent lake to survey,
We determined a walk to its banks we would take,
And therefore enquired the way to the lake.
Though the Sun, in his noon and meridian glory,
Was seeming to tell us a different story;
And that, if we attempted to walk to the lake,
Our faces he'd broil and our hands he would bake.
Now on by a path through the meadows we stray,
All rich with the fragrance of newly mown hay;

Each outracing the other, with much emulation
To arrive at the top of some small elevation ;
Till the sheet where the dark water still onward flows
Lay not at our feet but in front of our nose.
A shout burst from all, while each of us strove
He had first seen the blue billow rolling to prove,—
" I first saw the lake ! "—" No, no, no ! it was I ! "
Till mamma checked us all with a mum-making " fie ! "
We stood on the beach where some small piers of stone
Forth into the water some distance were thrown ;
While a fleet of small boats there at anchorage hung,
And dividing the ripples they carelessly swung.

But there on the beach,—and with shame be it said !—
Some women were washing,—oh, women indeed !—
Disfiguring the Derwent, their linen were washing,
And tubbing, and wetting, and splashing, and dashing.
They hung them all out on the boughs to be dried,
And clothed with a margin of linen the tide !
Oh, Jupiter ! dost thou in calmness yet see ?
Are the shores of the Derwent as nothing to thee ?—
Do these women not yet feel thy well-deserved rage ?
Oh, Jupiter, thou must be blinded with age !
Blind ? yes, quite stark blind from the length of thy life,
Or opposing the scolds of thy crabbed old wife.
It is a complete, a most excellent sign
That the all-seeing eye it no longer is thine.
But give, Jove, oh, give thy great, God-shaking frown,
And let on these women thine anger come down !

And now, having passed through a sun-shading wood,
On a point of rough rocks o'er the waters we stood.
The roots of the fir, of the elm, and the oak,
Through the rock-covering soil they a passage had broke ;
And oh ! they presented such nets for the toes,
We were always in danger of breaking our nose.
Below us, upon the dark wave-beaten rock,
The white, angry billows their foaming crests broke,
As soothing the ear with a ne'er ceasing dashing,
And moistening the moss and the weeds with their
      plashing.

And now some small height we did wish to attain,
A view of the lake and the valley to gain :
And so, in returning, turned off by a way
Which we thought tow'rd a tree-covered eminence lay.
It entered a wood ; we still kept going on,
Completely shut out from the light of the sun.
No part of the scene the confusèd eye sees,
Save copses on copses, and trees upon trees :
Till, the path in the forest bewilderingly tost,
All points of the compass completely were lost :
North, east, west, or south, from each other not knowing,
With all kinds of conjectures how, where we were going,
Although it afforded a great deal of fun.
"We shall soon find a path through the meadows," says
      one.—
"Lawkadaisy, that bough nearly knocked off my hat !"—
One of us says this, and another says that :

"We are nearing the lake, or at any rate ought to
     be ! "

"Well, I declare that a most excellent thought to be ! "

Thus wond'ring, we, serpent-like, twisted about,

Till just where we got in 'twas just there we got out.

And we this occurrence determined quite by

Not any more by-paths uncertain to try.

We left the fair lake where so azure it flowed, ·

And hotly set off by the Borrowdale road ;

And laughing, and chaffing, and gazing, and toiling,

Perspiring, and frying, and roasting, and broiling,

Glad, gladly the sheltering wood we surveyed,

Which promised to cool and to soothe with its shade.

The track it was steep, thorny, rugged and rocky,

As it angled and turned round the oak trees so
     knotty.

Some, decaying, were but a vast, grey, hollow shell ;

Of former young grandeur and might they did tell :

And the soil which hung thick round their huge roots
     far-spreading

Formed steps, trunk-supported, where'er we were treading.

We pulled up the hill, and we turned round about,

And we crossed and we recrossed within and without ;

To all parts of the wood we full pryingly rambled,

Over stone, over rock, we impatiently scrambled.

"Oh, we shall not get up to the summit this hour ! "—

"Oh, mamma, I have got such a beautiful flower ;

Here's a violet !   Look, mamma l pray, papa, do !

What is this of rich crimson ? this delicate blue ?

This moss of a bright living green do behold !
And here is a cowslip, the goblet of gold !
Look under the moss, there ; it cannot be sage !
What can that queer thing be ? ”—“ ’tis a saxifrage.”
“ And here’s Ladies Slipper, and here’s Ladies-smock
And this,”—“Oh don’t touch it, it’s poison,—Hemlock !”
And many more flowers ’mid the forest which grew,
Whose names I’ve forgot,—or perhaps never knew !
Now the rocks gave us rather more trouble to climb,
And rather more labour, and took us more time,
For the slippery moss always set us a-sliding,
Insomuch that we could not at all it confide in :
Except where, in velvety cushions, it grows,
And kindly invited our rock-fatigued toes.
“ These troublesome stones,—I am always a-stumbling !”
“ Hollo, what’s that there ?   I was nearly a-tumbling !”
“ What, do you not think we the summit are near ?”
“ Oh, give me your hand,—do pray help me up here !”
Till, emerging from under a thick, stunted tree,
An old rotten seat on the summit we see.
The people before to this summit who came
Had carved, or had hacked, on its surface their name,
And had covered the seat with no spaces between
　　　each,
Oh, mighty conceit,—so like Cockneys at Greenwich !
But ’twas so decrepid, so old and decayed,—
To trust to its legs we were somewhat afraid ;
Lest, tumbling as if we had sat upon wheels,
It had landed our heads in the place of our heels.

So some on a rock that was cushioned with moss,
And some on the June-tinted, brown turf repose;
Stretched out upon earth's verdant bosom we rest,
But tear her young flowers from her nourishing breast,
Which forth to our hands she luxuriantly poured :—
Thou sayest that it was but a cruel reward!

[HERO-WORSHIP.]

Now hurried we home, and while taking our tea
We thought—Mr. Southey at church we might see!
Next morning, the church how we wished to be
      reaching!
I'm afraid 'twas as much for the poet as preaching!
And, oh what a shame! were shown into a seat
With everything, save what was wanted, replete;
And so dirty, and greasy, though many times dusted,
The ladies all thought it could never be trusted;
First looking at seat, and again upon flounce,
And dusting, and gazing, for fear of their gowns!
I think all the time they took such mighty care
They sat upon thorns, and perhaps upon air!
Howe'er *I* forgave,—'deed, I scarcely did know it,—
For really we were 'cheek-by-jowl' with the poet!
His hair was no colour at all by the way,
But half of't was black, slightly scattered with grey;
His eyes were as black as a coal, but in turning
They flashed,—ay, as much as that coal does in burning!

His nose in the midst took a small outward bend,
Rather hooked like an eagle's, and sharp at the end ;
But his dark lightning-eye made him seem half inspired,
Or like his own Thalaba, vengefully fired.
We looked, and we gazed, and we stared in his face ;
Marched out at a slow-stopping, lingering pace ;
And as towards Keswick delighted we walked,
Of his face, and his form, and his features we talked.

[BORROWDALE IN A SHOWER.]

THE morning appeared with a great face of doubt,
Or to make us keep in, or to let us go out.
We look out of window,—call guides after guides,—
Demand whether rain or fair weather betides.
The first puts his thumb on one side of his nose,
And looks up to the smoke, to see how the wind
        blows ;
Then pronounces it after a great deal of puffing,
"A vara bad dai !   Why, you couldn't see nothing ! "
The next,—"Whai, ye sees, sir, I can't hardly say ;
Boot I'se think that it may be a middlin' fine day."
Another,—"For Skudda this never will do,
But I think's it prove fine, though not fit for a view ·
And so if you liked it, a trip you might take
By Borrowdale, down unto Bootthermere lake."
Delighted, we heard the most capital thought,
And at the glad prospect we eagerly caught.

By the road to dark Borrowdale onward we ride,

By the wave-beaten beach of the Derwent's blue tide.

But now we were roused by a few rainy pats

On the ribbon-bow'd bonnets, and crowns of the hats ·

Thus adding a fresh prospect unto the view,—

The beautiful prospect of being wet through !

So, covering our knees o'er with cloaks and shawls
     plenteous,

We erected a kind of a parasol pent-house.

Then, after a great deal of rain-preparation,

We awaited the shower, with a sad expectation.

It came with a kind of—"I do not know *what* to do !

What I should, what I could, what I would, what I ought
     to do !"

We were wondering much what 'twas going to be at,

And now it was this, and again it was that ;

And the rain it was changeable as was the wind,

Till to shine on our journey it made up its mind.

But the sun when at last to peep out he would deign,

Looked as if he'd been troubled as much by the rain,

And, vexed at the clouds so incessantly storming,

Looked as if he'd been crying the whole of the morning !

Now in front rose the cliff where, 'mid tumble and roar,

The quaking crags quiver 'neath angry Lodore.

But as long was the way, and as we were in haste,

Its waters,—those waters of thunder, we past.

And then we looked back upon Keswick's sweet vale,

Ere we entered the gorges of dark Borrowdale.

Beyond the bright space where the Derwent lake flows,
More majestic in distance huge Skiddaw arose;
And, softened, the valley was smilingly seen,
The lake's azure waters and islands between.
A range of huge mountains rose sheer from its verge,
And into the lake their steep pointlets they urge;
Where many a gulf, tree-surrounded, was made,
Where the wave placid rested, completely embayed:
While steep to the left the white Shepherd's crag
        stood,
And its loose slaty sides, thinly scattered with wood.

But now in our front our low road seemed to check
In a chaos of hills, a dark mountainous wreck;
Hanging o'er the dread dell their huge summits they
        hurled,
At whose feet the fair Derwent so crystalline purled.
Astonished we passed through that wilderness lone,
Till burst on our eyesight dark Bowder's huge stone.
A dark rock its high summit right forward did force,
And altered the fierce torrent's rock-beating course.
High raised on its brink, frowning down on the flood,
A vast mass of mossy rock dreadfully stood:
It seemed from the hills high above as if torn,
And down to its wonderful resting-place borne.
But nature most queerly contrived has to hitch it,
And poised on a narrow edge managed to pitch it.
As when some vast ship the blue ocean divides,
Her keen arching bow stems the breast of the tides;

The wondering waves 'gainst her stern dash their spray ;
The waters enraged yet are forced to obey ;
And back from her sides the huge billows are thrown :—
So sternly triumphing appeared Bowder Stone.

[HONISTAR CRAG.]

AND now on the peak of the mountain we stood,—
Looked back upon field, upon forest, and flood.
Where sun-topped Helvellyn his summits upthrew,
Distinctly outlined on the firmament blue ;
And the few retired fields, which in Borrowdale lay,
So richly reposed in th' enlivening ray.
But no longer we now on the mountain remain,
But hasten broad Buttermere's banks to attain :
Our way down the gorge of the valley we bend,
And slowly the rough mountain-path we descend.
Vast Honistar Crag, overhanging the road,
Pushed right 'cross our path his high forehead so
        broad,
Opposing our progress.   We turned round his brow,—
Encircled his cliff by the streamlet below ;
And gazed on the giant, as round him we wheeled,
As his wonderful shape was distinctly revealed.
He's none of your beauties,—no elegant wood
With romantical glades on his summit upstood ;
No "softening the scene," or "enlivening the view,"
No "fading in distance the mountains so blue : "

No Cockneys could find in its dread rock so antique
The fair picturesque or the rural romantic;
No silly school-bred miss just turned seventeen
Can affectedly say of 't—"How charming a scene!!!"
But above any misses, O my admiration!—
Dark Honistar Crag rears his stern elevation.

[THUNDERSTORM AT BUTTERMERE.]

BUT now on the mountains the dark clouds assembled,
And the waves of the lake they more gloomily trembled;
And then came a calm on its billowless breast,
As deep expectation were stilling its rest.
The air was oppressive, and sultry, and still,
And no cooling breezes swept over the hill.
When lo! from a cloud o'er dark Honistar's head
There gleamed through the darkness a thunderbolt red.
The lake for a moment reflected the flash,
Then dreadfully heard in the distance a crash,
As if mountains on mountains that moment were hurled,
Or dashed into atoms and ruins a world,
Or rocks to their heart by the lightning were riven,—
So the thunder it rolled o'er the face of the heaven.
Re-echoing from mountains, rebounding from hills,
Again the dread sound the vast æther it fills:
O'er gloomy Helvellyn sublimely it swells,
Then wakes the rude echoes of Langdale's peaked fells;
The thunder it spoke from the crags of Lodore,
And Skiddaw's twin summits awoke to the roar.

Then, fitful, the breeze from its mountainous hold
Forced all the stern thunders to peace as it rolled.
The winds in their anger rushed down on the deep,
Through every ravine, with a passionate sweep;
Then woke the dark waters, and plumage of foam
On the lake's swelling bosom was dazzlingly thrown,
Reflecting the lightning; and rattling peals
Again roused the mimicking sport of the hills.
Those chasm-hidden lions again from their caves
Sent back the dread sounds o'er the wondering waves;
And the echoes from Black-combe, o'erhanging the main,
To Sca-fell in mockery growled them again.
And numberless flashes and numberless roars
Hurled all their lone terrors on deep Crummock's shores;
Till the clouds, o'er the lake which so threateningly hung,
Flew away, the huge fells of the Derwent among.

Then first, the bright orb of the heavens appearing,
Again with his presence the hills he was cheering;
Though a shower, yet distilling its dews on the ground,
Its glistering drops was outpouring around.
Till, high o'er the heads of the mountains below,
There spanned the wide heavens the wonderful bow;
All glowing in purple, and crimson, and gold,
It grasped in its circle the waters, which rolled,—
Returning the colours so gloriously given,—
Returning again to the face of the heaven.

[MYTHOLOGICAL METEOROLOGY.]

THE morning was lovely : the bright azure sky
With light, fleecy clouds it was studded on high,
As if Jupiter's sheep from their fold they had strayed,
And o'er their blue meadows a ramble had made.
Perhaps you will say that the gods had no sheep !
Sir, I will not enter on argument deep.
But this I will say that you must recollect, sir,
That their goblets of gold were filled brimful of nectar ·
And this to th' opinion perhaps may give rise,—
They had plenty of nectarine trees in the skies !
And as to their having a good flock of sheep,—
If they drank, I should think they had something to eat :
And, although if they didn't, I care not a button,
The gods lived on *something;* oh, why not on mutton ?

[ULLSWATER ; A DIGRESSION.]

Now were I,—oh, were I a proper lake-poet
—Although you will say, " 'Tis in vain, that ;"—I know it!
But I cannot do what I know that I should,—
Pop in an address to the nymph Solitude.
Oh, beautiful,—beautiful should my muse make her,
With a " thou " and a " thee " like the words of a Quaker,
All so fine.—" Thou companion of Night, the black -
　　brow'd,
Who spreads o'er all Nature her star-spangled shroud——"

'Tis in vain,—'tis in vain ! I am *not* a lake-poet !
I knew from the first on't that I couldn't do it,
Oh, pray, oh Melpomene, help me up here !
I never shall do for the fashion, I fear ·
Spite of all the endeavour by poor me that made is,
I shall miss the applause of the misses and ladies.
For contrary unto the laws that are writ
In nature's own code, every Miss makes a hit
At poor me and my rhymes, for they're not sentimental,
And so to the—stop !—to oblivion they're sent all.
But the poets forget, when they praise Solitude,
That by rights upon her they should never intrude ;
And therefore, if truly and rightly 'twere known,
They praise her the best when they let her alone.

But I am digressive ! Oh, pray, do not blame me !
In description I know it would go on but lamely.
You know that description alone—it would be, sir,
A tedious thing that would tire you and me, sir.
You'd find, sir, in spite of the Grand and Sublime
A little Ridiculous wanting in time.
It's all very well to address Melancholy,
And the Night, and the Morning, and other such folly ;
Or a sonnet to night-loving, fair Philomel,
In a fine lady's album these look very well.
But though you may think me prodigiously assical
I do like some fun—something that's Hudibrastical.
Let every pert miss interrupt me in middle,
With a proper, school-bred, and genteel kind of giggle—

" I, I "—oh, dear me !—But I'll make a confession
—I'm digressive when I do but talk of digression.

'Tis enough : I go on.   By the banks of the lake
Towards fair Patterdale we our progress did take;
[Still] hoping each house that we saw on before
Would turn out the inn on the waves' woody shore :
Though we wondering saw that our horses did trot
To the lake's extreme end, and that still we stopped not.
And when full half a mile from its verge we advance,
Despair threw our minds in a wondering trance.
And certes not less than that distance we drive,
Until at the house, or the inn, we arrive.

Now, though I be called an egregious sinner,
I had not forgot at Ullswater my dinner.
In the good open air it is well to be lunching,
—You always see scenery best when you're munching.
You'd think the view beautiful, if in his hand each
'Tween finger and thumb had a mustarded sandwich :
The mutton alive, which away from you fled,
Would look better if you had a little on't dead.
Remember old Skiddaw !   The sandwiches there
Drove off all the cold of the rarefied air !
Can one relish a view without any provision—
Not at all fortified with the beef-ammunition ?
Impossible !   'Tis very well, sir, for you,
Who a good appetite, sir, perhaps never knew !

[COMING DOWN FROM KIRKSTONE.]

OH, then was a time when we gazèd once more
Upon Windermere's woody and waving shore;
On the gloomy ravine where we first saw the stream
Dash down those rude rocks 'mid that mountainous
      dream;
On the smoke which curled up to a slight elevation
From the tree-buried lum of the inn "Salutation;"
On the bridge over which lay our Keswick-bound track,
When we left the fair scene to which now we came back
On the house which we saw from our darling Low-wood—
By the bye, 'twas a beautiful nook where it stood:
'Twas snugly embayed by the side of the lake,
Just where the two rivers do into it break.
I'd like such a house:—and yet, no,—I would not:
There's a circumstance I had completely forgot;
If these gingerbread houses—there now are but few,
And they rather improve, not disfigure the view,—
But I say, if these things were allowed to increase,
And disturb in that landscape its own native peace,
No longer 'twould be all so lovelily lone,
And the mightiness, silence, and grandeur be gone.

But, reader, I'm slow, and you'll go on without me:
I was in a parenthesis, looking about me!
We gazed upon all that there was to be seen,—
On the lake that was blue,—on the fields that were
      green,—

On the dome of the sky, of such mighty extension,
And other small things that we needn't here mention.
But we stayed not our steps, for, the chariot entering,
We soon to our Low-wood were rapidly cantering.
And gallantly, gallantly onward we bore,
Till the driver reined up all our steeds at the door.
Bobbed out Mrs. Jackson with " How d'ye do, sir?
I hope you're quite well ; and miss, madam, and you, sir?
Your beds are all aired, and your rooms are all ready.
These horses are troublesome ;—steady, Jack, steady!
The flies do so tease them.　But pray, sir, come in ;
It soon will be raining, sir ; do come within !"
And then to our parlour and bedrooms she brought us,
And we, very happily, took up our quarters.
Now, reader, I spare thee ! at length will my pen
Its galloping course condescend to rein in ·
For while the short week that I was not a rover
Full many adventures and things I pass over.
Let's see :—I could tell more than ever you'd read, sir ;
So I'll give ye one pleasant excursion instead, sir.

[EXCURSION TO CONISTON.]

THE people of Low-wood one opening day
Intended to cut for the horses the hay :
And said, when a moment the sun chose to shine,
That they were quite certain the day would be fine.
We trusted to them ; they, again, to the sky
Which told, or which looked, an egregious lie !

Quite prepared for the rain, but yet caring no less,
We thundered all off on the road to Bowness.
The lake, like the tale of the bear and the fiddle,
Is almost cut off by two capes in the middle.
That the waters may not bar the path of the rover,
A kind of a hobblety boat paddles over;
And, in order to urge on its clumsiness fast,
They've got a huge oar that might do for a mast:
And, what is much worse, they have *not* got a sail,
That might catch in its foldings the breath of the gale.
So, o'er the dark waters they lump and they lumber,
And over the lake they do bump and they blunder;
With us all behind, and the horses before,
And the coach in the centre, we get to the shore.
They tumbled us out as they bundled us in,
At the risk of immersing us up to the chin:
And instead of us paying, sir, they in a trice
Demanded and asked an exorbitant price!
But we could not avoid it,—so, paid it; and then
We galloped by mountain, and torrent, and glen.

But although the wide heavens kept fair for a while,
Yet, ere we had passed by much more than a mile,
In lowering aspect began they to frown.
Then,—then,—"Well, what then?"—then the shower
        came down!
"Oh, is *that* all?"—Dear sir, pray what *would* you have
        more?
"Oh, that's quite enough; but I knew it before."

What, did you, sir? Dear me, 'twas much more than *I*
     did ;
I knew not at all how it would be decided.
But anyhow, now, the decision's a bad one
To pepper us—'deed, a prodigiously sad one.
We groaned in our hearts, but we did not complain,
When we knew, if we did so, the more it would rain.
We looked on the mountains obscured by the cloud ;
We looked on the streams from their summits which
     flowed,
And, down into Coniston's waters careering,
With furrows full deep the dark mountains were searing ;
No outlines were seen of their rock-broken form,
All darkly obscured by the mist and the storm.
And the birds sang not now to the murmuring floods,
For each of them fled to his home in the woods ;
And the torrents in cataracts fiercely did pour,
And to their wild roaring re-echoed the shore ;
And bent to the force of the wind every tree
As that tempest was pouring its own melodie.

Although it was placed in a fine situation,
The inn did not equal our anticipation ;
It might be the day,—and I will not deny it,—
For really the lake was most beautiful by it.
Of fair-weather prophecies mind you be wary,
For the day made old Coniston look solitary :
And, what made it worse, we had nothing to do,
Save watching the course of the clouds as they flew,

Or counting the ripples that rolled to the strand,
Or looking where lingered the slow minute-hand.
Sometimes we looked up at the troublesome sky,
And peeped through the breaks of the clouds, riding by;
Though we saw that they rather grew darker than
       thinner,—
Till a respite appeared in the entrance of dinner.

When dinner was over, as still it did rain,
We thought that we scarcely need longer remain :
So, ordered the carriage, and with no good will,
We ordered that pest of all travels—the bill.
May the money bear witness how quickly they made it!
—Much quicker than we were inclined to have paid it.
Though, without further grumbling, the silver we gave,
And galloped away from old Coniston's wave.

Yet, ere we should leave it in tempest and rain,
We, turning, looked back on its waters again.
All open and bare they, full lonely, did lie,
Exposing their breast to the shadowy sky :
Retiring in distance they mistily lay ;
And fainter each inlet, and softer each bay ;
Till, appearing no more, by the wild tempest tost,
'Mid mountains and clouds in the distance were lost.
These mountains, all mistily softened away,
Appeared like thin clouds at the dawn of the day ;
Still darker and deeper, in bolder relief,
As, nearer approaching, and rising the chief,

The mighty Old Man, with his dark summit r
Closing the prospect arose on our left.

Farewell to the lake, and farewell to the mou
The tarn, and the torrent,—the fall, and the
To the deeps of the dell, and the wood-shade
Thou land of the mountains, I see thee no m

.

I wanderd forth at midnight
And silently silently rove
Where the moonlight poured
On the dewy sward
And on the elfin grove
Twas a kind of farry scenery
A kind of arry dreamery
Such silence as I love

When from the wood around me
The elfin circles skim
Hand in hand
They join the band
And in the dances swim
And there they bounded merrily
While sailing round me giddily
And breezy numbers sing

How softly softly murmuring
In sinking cadence low
And now they seem
Of joy to sing
And now to   of woe

Those carols greet me listening
And harmoniously flow

Thus ran the song Ye fairies
Now swiftly swiftly bound
Ere yet the day
In twilight gray
Shall shed its light around
Spring oer the dewdrop shivering
Touch not the grassblade quivering
While vaulting from the ground

Still circling on the green sward
Exert your nimble feet
Dance dance away
Ye fairies gay
And Joly your footsteps fleet
Ye sprites ye elfins wantoning
Amongst the cowslips frolicking
Here let your dances meet   IR

TO MY HEART.

WHY leapest thou,
Why leapest thou
So high within my breast?
Oh, stay thee now,
Oh, stay thee now,
Thou little bounder, rest!

2.

"I will not stay,
I will not stay,
For nought but joy I know;
For I must stay
On a future day,
Not ignorant, *then*, of woe.

3.

"Oh, let me leap,
Oh, let me leap,
Till that sad day shall come,

When thou shalt weep
In sorrow deep
For days of gladness gone."

4.

Oh, say not so,
Oh, say not so,
My heart, Oh, do not say,
That bitter draught
Shall e'er be quaffed—
Shall e'er be drained by me!

5.

"And shalt thou not
Know mankind's lot,
Shalt thou from it be free?
In future years
That lot of tears
Shall fix itself on thee.

6.

"Then let me leap,
Then let me leap,
Till that dread day shall come,
When thou shalt weep
In anguish deep
For paths of pleasure run.

7.

"When age is come
And youth is done—
That youth so briefly given,—
Then thou shalt trust
No more in dust
Fix thy hope on heaven.

26 *January.*

TO POESIE.

Oh, what art thou,—Oh, what art thou,
  Thou thing of living fire?
The laurels are twined around thy brow,
  And thy hand is on the lyre,
Which breathes such notes of harmony
As make the young heart lighter leap,
And with greater rapture beat:
  Oh, what art thou?

Thou art a thing of nothingness,
  Thou art fancy's wayward child;
Thou art a thing of brightest bliss;
Thy lips are breathing happiness,
  In thy numbers wandering wild.

Thou art the burstings of the heart,
  The language of the fiery soul;
    Thou art nature's voice and tone:

While as thy numbers higher roll,
In mystic harmony,
 With soundings all thine own.

4.

When the brightest gems of heaven
 Pour their radiance on earth,
  And all are lost in sleep,
  Then thou, then thou dost sweep
The chords of thine impassioned lyre,
 And unto thoughts and images give birth,
And pour thy lay unto the listening moon,
 And fill the heavens with harmony
  As pure, as high as they.

5.

When the wave doth madly fling
His spray, and the thunders roll in heaven,
  And the lightnings illumine the deep,
  And the tempests wildly sweep;
Then thou dost cast thy numbers
 Upon their angry wing;
Mingle thy voice with the thunders,
And notes of woe, and notes of dread,
 In various lyrics sing.

March 11.

WANT OF A SUBJECT.

1.

I WANT a thing to write upon,
But I cannot find one;
And I have wanted one so long
That I must write on—none l

2.

I think of speeches to the sea,—
Its colour azure blue,
And all its moaning minstrelsy,—
That a'n't it,—that won't do!

3.

I think of speeches to the ground,
And all its flowers too,
And all the treasures in it found,—
That a'n't it,—that won't do !

4.

I think of speeches to the sky,—
Its far expanse so blue,
And all its starry majesty,—
That a'n't it,—that won't do !

5.

I think of Saturday's dread night,
   Its apparatus too,
Beside its bason blue and white,—
   That a'n't it,—that won't do!

6.

Think of the poultry; how the cock
   To's dames the morsel threw;
How to the dainty bit they flock,—
   That a'n't it,—that won't do!

7.

I think of New-Year's-day, replete
   With joys and pleasures new,
When parties gay with parties meet—
   That a'n't it,—that won't do!

8.

Though many, many, many a thing
   Doth flit my brain about,
As quickly as they scamper in,
   So quickly they're.kicked out!

9.

And following thoughts on thoughts so fleet,
   But still none of them suit;
And I—I am almost asleep,
   And still my muse is mute.

10.

And lest she urge her airy flight
From my so drowsy brain,
Upon *no* subject I will write,
That so she may remain.

[*About March.*]

TO THE OCEAN SPIRITS.

YE, who dwell in the coral caves,
　　Where the billows ever sleep;
Ye, who ride on the briny waves,
　　Spirits of the deep—
Of the mighty and dark and unsearchable deep—
　　Hither, come hither all!
Glide ye and sail ye and sport ye there,
Mermaids all with golden hair?
Or do ye silence the sounding sea,—
Do ye sing him to sleep with your melody?
Do ye lie on the weedy rocks so cold,
Where the greedy surge has ever rolled?
Or braid ye your flowing hair with pearls,
Strewing them all in the golden curls?
　　Hither, come hither all!
Mingle your voices with the sea,
Sing me a joyous melody.
Let the waves from your breath rebounding
Dash on the vocal rocks resounding.
Now is the hour ere the red sun bathes
　　His sides in the rosy deep;
Ere he nods his head to the laughing waves,
　　To his rolling couch of sleep.

MERMAIDS (*sing*).

We are capricious ocean's daughters,
Children of the inconstant waters ;
In our coral caverns, we
Live in mirth and minstrelsy :
Sport we all in depths unknown,
In places silent, dark and lone.
We have seen the dead man's skull
With pearly shells and seaweeds full ;
But ever he grasped with convulsive hold
The chest where lay the mouldy gold.
Oh, well we love to swim the deep,
And cut the foam so fast and fleet ;
While Tritons with the vocal shell
In our train their music swell.
The very sharks lift up their head
From crunching and crashing the bones of the dead ;
And, as we pass them swiftly by,
List to the shelly harmony.

Enough, enough ! the song is done ;
Sinks beneath the deep the sun,
        Down, down, down,
To the depths of the ocean down.
Away, away, ye nymphs, away !
Darkness shrouds the closing day.

20 *June.*

TO THE FAIRIES.

YE, who sport in the lone midnight,
By the paly round moon's flickering light :
Ye, who dance in your forests lone,
Till the pale glow-worm lights you home,
    Hither, come hither all !
Do ye sing to the nightingale ?
Do ye lie in a cowslip's bell ?
Or do ye drink from the acorn-cups
The dew ye love so well ?
Ere the day, the rosy day,
   From forth its couch shall rise,
And throw aside its mantle grey
   For a red one in the skies,
    Hither, come hither all !
And, like the gentle, peaceful dove,
Who to his mate now coos his love ;
Or like the plaintive nightingale,
Who telleth now his lonely tale,
Sing ye your carols unto me
With midnight mirth and melody.

FAIRIES (*sing*).

Evil spirits, black and dun,
To our revels do not come,
In the church-yards dark and lone,
By the pale, inscriptioned stone.
Fly ye from this sacred ground,
Nor be in our circles found!
Riding on the grey bat's wings,
Hum ye from our dancing-rings
　　Away, away, away!
Oh, how we love to sport us now,
When all unclouded is the brow
Of the bright, benignant moon
'Mid a half-enlightened gloom;
And every tree doth bend its head,
As lightly o'er the grass we tread;
And, as we dance on dewy mounds,
They list to hear the jocund sounds
That whisper round their aged roots.
For oh, we love to lie 'mid flowers,
And sleep amid the violets,
Until the dawning hours.
Till the sun lights the morning dew
That glisters on the ground,
Amid the forests we are found,
Frolicking all the woodlands through!
　　Stay, stay, stay!
The dawn upon the hills appears,

The dew shines on the grass like tears.
At the approach of day
    Silence !
Vanish, every elf and fay !

20 June.

"Now go, my dear.   'Tis time to go to bed."
      Oh, direful sentence ; all so full of woe !
Oh dear ! how mournfully those words are said,
      —So contradictory,—" *Come*, dear, and *go !* "
When anything had come into my head
      To all composing 'tis the fiercest foe.
I wish Mamma a little less would load us
With so much of *imperativus modus*.

When Mr. —— What d'ye call him ?—Bottom-roe ?
      No, that's not it . . . Oh ay, it is Roebotham—
Has ceased his parallelograms to show
      And t'other thingumbobs—I have forgot 'em !
With latitude and longitude, you know,
      And all the other things there's such a lot on,
Why, then I cannot have a little play, sir ;
For, "Go away to bed" Mamma doth say, sir.

When I have drudged all day at dry perspective,
      And some nice clever book I have begun,
Against those words there must be no invective,—
      I cannot have a little bit of fun ;

For of the time Mamma's so recollective,
　　You might as well attempt to cheat the sun !
And nothing pleasant can I then begin it,
Mamma so regularly counts each minute !

[*About September.*]

[TO THE MEMORY OF SIR WALTER SCOTT.]

'Twas night.   I stood by Tweed's fair stream.
Methought it sang a dirge for him
Who once on its green borders drew
The fanciful, the fairy crew:
And seemed a voice, in measured tone,
To breathe a melancholy moan.
And, whispering, sullen soundings sighed,
As mingling with the murmuring tide;
And sorrowing notes of woe they gave,
As floating on the mystic wave.
And, with the waters borne along,
They joined with every zephyr's song.
The billows wept that they no more,
When rolling tow'rds the hallowed shore,
Might dance into the living lays
That minstrel's magic voice could raise;
Where every mocking mountain rang
With the rich numbers that he sang;

Where piny forests, when he spoke,
Their hoary locks in wonder shook ;
And bent their spiry heads, when he
Charmed Scotland's hills with harmony.

October.

[THE ETERNAL HILLS.]

I LOVE ye, ye eternal hills,
  With the mists all wreathed around ye;
I love ye, all ye cloud-born rills,
  As ye beat the rocks that bound ye.
I've seen ye when the huge storm-fiend
  From his peaceful sleep doth rouse,
And the misty coronet doth bind
  On your mighty, shaggèd brows;
      A thing of might
      In his gloomy flight,
  As he buries ye, hills, in his stormy night.

I love ye, I love ye, mighty things,
  With your huge and frowning fells;
When the eagle flaps his nervous wings,
  And the tempest round ye swells.
I've seen ye with your forests hoar,
  As they nod o'er your crags all lone,
And your crags do shake 'neath the torrent's roar,

And are snowed with rock-borne foam
As they wake from their sleep
When those waters leap
Into your caverns dark and deep.

[*About October.*]

THE SITE OF BABYLON.

THE desert stretched its ocean sweep,
All vast and boundless as the deep
   In mighty solitude;
Night, like a lion o'er his prey,
Above the vast, the desert way,
   In silence stern did brood.
I stood beside one tree that flung
A gloomy shadow, where it hung;
And not a column,—not a stone—
Marked out the site of Babylon.

2.

Where art thou now, thou haughty one
Whose mighty walls so often rung
   With the proud feasts of kings?
And foaming wine in golden bowls
Has flowed, where now the lion prowls
   And the hoarse night-breeze sings.

Alas ! that mightiness is fled,
Barbaric pomp is witherèd ;
And o'er the eastern glory's grave
Euphrates rolls his gloomy wave.

6 November.

[MOONLIGHT ON THE MOUNTAINS.˥

1.

CURTAINED in cloudy drapery
The stars were glimmering on high,
All with a light festoonery
Round their fulgent centre queen,
Fleecily, as veiled between
Sate she, and with them did roll
Round the fixed, eternal pole.

2.

Folding, like an airy vest,
The very clouds had sunk to rest ;
Light gilds the rugged mountain's breast,
Calmly as they lay below ;
Every hill seemed topped with snow,
As the flowing tide of light
Broke the slumbers of the night.

30 *November.*

SONNET.

HARLECH CASTLE.

I'VE seen thy mighty towers and turrets high,
   Like crown imperial on some rocky head,
   'Mid the eternal hills so darkly spread
Round the huge Snowdon's mountain-majesty,
Shunning the earth, enamoured of the sky,—
   Ruined remembrance of the silent dead,
   Now sleeping in a mountain-guarded bed,
That once did stir these walls with revelry.

And all and aught that once was great is gone!
   Doth the cold ivy round thy ruins fling
Its twining arms to clothe the naked stone ·
   Flaps round the keep the lazy owlet's wing.
—So mighty, so majestic, and so lone!
   —And all thy music, now, the ocean's murmuring!

[*End of* 1831.]

SONNET TO A CLOUD.

THOU little roamer of the northern blast,
    Mantling the brow of ruby-fringèd morn,
    So swift, so transient,—whither art thou borne?
Hither and thither by the breezes cast,
Hast shadowed sultry Araby, or past—
    Lumed by the lightning—on the gloomy storm?
    Or dimmed the lustre of the moonè's horn?
Or swept o'er mountain-summit, fleet and fast?
Or darkened o'er the bosom of the brine?
    Or, wanton, fled the summer breeze's sigh,
And floated o'er a thirsty, scorching clime,
    Fading upon the clear and azure sky?
—Methinks I see thee, like the wing of time
    Melting away into Eternity!

[*End of* 1831.]

AT 13 YEARS OF AGE.

SONNET TO THE MORNING (*Feb.* 5).
THE SONG OF THE SOUTHERN BREEZE (*Feb.* 12).
THE DESTRUCTION OF PHARAOH. [*about March*].
THE GRAVE OF THE POET (*September*).

SONNET

TO THE MORNING.

SEE, where she comes, the mountain-mists of night
   Scarce yet unwreathing their fantastic shapes
   Of pinnacle and tower, when morn awakes
Fainter and fainter in confusing flight
Leave hill and vale, all wrapt in rosy light.
   She comes : she looks upon the silent lakes ;
   The last long-lingering cloud the hill forsakes
Far in the clear blue sky that heaves his height.

The choral choirs that people every tree
   Join with the music of the stream, that flows
Adown the mountain-side with jocund glee.
   There is a simple softness in those lays
That wakes the heart of man to piety,
   To hymn his Father's, his Creator's praise.

(*Feb.* 5.)

THE SONG OF THE SOUTHERN BREEZE.

OH, what is the voice of the wind that flies
All by the waste and wintry skies?
What is the voice of the breeze that swells
Down by the darksome and dreary dells?
Where has it been,
And what has it seen,
As it sailed, the high crest of the billows between?
Sweeping the heather that girdles the mountain,
And circling the waves as they foam on the fountain.
For the tempest-child
It singeth so wild
'Mongst the hills that are heavenward piled;—
"Lullaby, lullaby!"
Has it sung above the wave;—
"Lullaby, lullaby!"
O'er the sailor's ocean-grave.
Where hast thou been
By the ocean green?
Tell me, wild wind, where thou hast been?

BREEZE.

I have come from the southern land,
All by India's pearly strand;

And the spicy gales they were following me,
As I swept across the boundless sea.
I have raised the flag of the war-ship's mast,
As it hung down lazilie;
I have sung my song with the midnight blast,
With a mournful melodie.
Oh, I have gone so fleet and fast,
By the rocks of the sounding sea;
And the waves, they smiled as I by them past,
And they smiled with their foam on me.
I have fanned the skies of Araby,
Across the lonely sand;
And I have seen the pilgrim die
In a far and foreign land.
I've seen full many a mountain-height
Uprear his giant form of might;
And I have flown
By the desert lone,
By Chimborazo's mountain-throne.
I have borne the red bolt on my breast,
As it fiercely crackled by;
I have lulled the ocean into rest,
With my soft and soothing sigh.
I have caught the clouds from the golden west
Where the sun delights to die;
And I've been by the crags of the mountain's crest,
That reareth himself on high.
E'en now there's a cloud that is waiting for me,
To carry him over the northern sea.

I must away—
Over the ocean away,—
Full far and full far I must urge my flight;
Ere that day shall be drowned in the mists of t
I am gone by the crests of foam and snow
That hide the waters' depth below,
Away, and away!

February 12.

[THE DESTRUCTION OF PHARAOH.]

MOURN, Mizraim, mourn! The weltering wave
Wails loudly o'er Egyptia's brave
  Where lowly laid they sleep;
The salt sea rusts the helmet's crest;
The warrior takes his ocean-rest,
  Full far below the deep.
—The deep, the deep, the dreary deep!
—Wail, wail, Egyptia! mourn and weep!
For many a mighty legion fell
Before the God of Israël.

Wake, Israel, wake the harp. The roar
Of ocean's wave on Mizraim's shore
  Rolls now o'er many a crest.
Where, now, the iron chariot's sweep?
Where Pharaoh's host? Beneath the deep
  His armies take their rest.
Shout, Israel! Let the joyful cry
Pour forth the notes of victory;
High let it swell across the sea,
For Jacob's weary tribes are free!

[*About March*].

[THE GRAVE OF THE POET.]

THE grass grows green on the banks of Tweed,
The river rolls clear over pebble and weed ;
The wave is bright, and the foam is light,
All in the eddies gurgling white.
Shall the grass grow green on the banks of Tweed
When the grave has seized its lord ?
Shall the river roll clear over pebble and weed
When he lies 'neath the cold green-sward ?
Heavily lieth the sod on his breast,
Low is his pillow and long his rest ;
Cold on his grave may the moonbeam shiver,—
The soul of the minstrel is parted for ever !
Doth he lie on the mountain-heath
Where the tempest sings his dirge of death ?
Or is his shroud
The misty cloud,
Clothing the cliffs that are rising proud ?
Meet were a grave so waste and wild,
Meet for the grave of a mountain-child !
Shall the cloistered pile receive him,
Where the ivy round is weaving ?
Where shall he be laid ?
Where his last sad requiem said ?

For the ivy's enwreathing
The harp and the chord,
And the worm is entwining
The brow of the bard.

September.

1833.

AT 14 YEARS OF AGE.

SONG.

I WEARY for the torrent leaping
From off the scar's rough crest;
My muse is on the mountain sleeping,
My harp is sunk to rest.

I weary for the fountain foaming,
For shady holm and hill;
My mind is on the mountain roaming,
My spirit's voice is still.

I weary for the woodland brook
That wanders through the vale;
I weary for the heights that look
Adown upon the dale.

The crags are lone on Coniston,
And Loweswater's dell;
And dreary on the mighty one,
The cloud-enwreathed Sca-fell.

Oh! what although the crags be stern
Their mighty peaks that sever,
Fresh flies the breeze on mountain fern,
And free on mountain heather.

I long to tread the mountain head
Above the valley swelling;
I long to feel the breezes sped
From grey and gaunt Helvellyn.

I love the eddying, circling sweep,
The mantling and the foam
Of murmuring waters dark and deep,
Amid the valleys lone.

It is a terror, yet 'tis sweet,
Upon some broken brow
To look upon the distant sweep
, Of ocean spread below.

There is a thrill of strange delight
That passes quivering o'er me,
When blue hills rise upon the sight
Like summer clouds before me.

[*Winter*, 1832-3.]

MY FATHER'S BIRTHDAY.

THE month of May, the month of May,
I love it for its jocund hours;
The merry hours that fly away
As swiftly as its flowers.
I love it for the laugh so light
It throws o'er all the face of nature,
A something gladdening and bright
That glistens on her every feature.
I see it where the grass grows green
On daisied mead, by sparkling stream;
I hear it in the roundelay
The birds pour forth at dawn of day.

The brook that to and fro meanders
Bears gladness in its crystal springs;
There's gladness in the wind that wanders
Among the hawthorn-blossomings.
But doubly pure each glancing stream,
More gaily decked each tree,
And brighter every noontide beam,
And lovelier to me,—

More deeply blue thy sky above,—
More soft each songster's lay of love,—
For in thy blooming month, fair May,
I hail my father's natal day !

10th May.

ACCOUNT OF A TOUR ON THE CONTINENT.

"Early in the spring of 1833 Prout published his Sketches in Flanders and Germany. I well remember going with my father into the shop where subscribers entered their names, and being referred to the specimen print, the turreted window over the Moselle, at Coblentz. We got the book home to Herne Hill before the time of our usual annual tour; and as my mother watched my father's pleasure and mine in looking at the wonderful places, she said, why should we not go and see some of them in reality? My father hesitated a little, then with glittering eyes said—why not? And there were two or three weeks of entirely rapturous and amazed preparation. . . .

"We went by Calais and Brussels to Cologne; up the Rhine to Strasburg, across the Black Forest to Schaffhausen, then made a sweep through North Switzerland by Basle, Berne, Unterlachen, Lucerne, Zurich, to Constance,—following up the Rhine still to Coire, then over Splügen to Como, Milan, and Genoa; meaning, as I now remember, for Rome. But, it being June already, the heat of Genoa warned us of imprudence: we turned, and came back over the Simplon to Geneva, saw Chamouni, and so home by Lyons and Dijon." (*Præterita*, I. iv.)

CALAIS.

THE sands are in the sunlight sleeping,
[The tide upon the bar is leaping;]
Again, again for evermore
Haste the light curlings to the shore,

And yet advance and yet retreat
On playful childhood's daring feet,
That seeks within its sandy cell
The pebble bright, or purple shell.
Far in its clear expanse, lay wide
Unruffledly that ocean tide,
Stretching away where paler grew
The heaven's bright unclouded blue.
And, far away in distance dying,
Old England's cliffy coast was lying;
And beautiful as summer cloud
By the low sun empurpled proud.

Strange, that a space from shore to shore
So soon, so easily passed o'er,
Should yet a wide distinction place
'Twixt man and man, 'twixt race and race!
Sudden and marked the change you find,—
Religion, language, even mind;
That you might think that narrow span
Marked the varieties of man.

CASSEL.

THE way was long, and yet 'twas sweet,—
Through many a shady, soft retreat,
Where the broad willow semblance gave
Of weeping beauty to the wave;
And elm, with massy foliage prest,
And feathery aspen's quivering crest;

And many a spiry poplar glade,
And hazel's rich entangled shade :
While, onward as advancing still
From Omer's plain to Cassel's hill,
Far—yet more far the landscape threw
Its deep, immeasurable blue.
Oh, beautiful those plains were showing,
Where summer sun was hotly glowing !
Many a battlefield lay spread—
Once the dark dwelling of the dead :
But fruitful now their champaigns wave
With bending grain on soldier's grave.
While far beneath in long array
The priestly orders wound their way ;
Heavy the massive banners rolled,
Rich wrought with gems, and stiff with gold :
While, as the cross came borne on high
Beneath its crimson canopy,
Many the haughty head that bowed,—
Sunk his high crest the warrior proud,
The priest his glance benignant cast,
And murmured blessings as he past ;
While, round the hillside echoing free,
Rung the loud-hymning melody.
Many a monkish voice was there,—
Many a trumpet rent the air,—
And softer, sweeter, yet the same,
The sounds in failing cadence came.

LILLE.

OH, red the blushing east awoke,
And bright the morn on Cassel broke ;
Along the green hillside we flew ;
Flashed the clear sunshine in the dew
That on the clustering herbage hung,—
That to the tangled copsewood clung,—
That shot like stars through every shade,
And glanced on every wildwood glade.
At length, by many a wind descending
That ever to the plain were bending
Farther, and farther still, we pressed
From Cassel's insulated crest,
That, back retiring, fainter still
Showed the rich outlines of its hill,
And faded in the purple haze
That spoke the coming noontide blaze.
That noontide blaze delayed not long ;
On Tournay's tow'rs 'twas fierce and strong,
And, ere we gained the middle way,
The glow was like an Afric day.
Full upon Lille's high ramparts round,
On massive wall and moated mound,
Shot the fierce sun his glaring ray,
As bent we on our burning way :
Till past the narrow drawbridge-length—
The massive gates' portcullised strength,

And moat, whose waves found steepy shore
Where forward huge the bastion bore;
And where the sentinels were set
High on the dizzy parapet:
Till the last portal's echoes woke,
And Lille upon us sudden broke,
Giving to view another scene,
So clear, so noble, so serene,
'Twould seem enchantment's varied hue
On palace, street, and avenue.
Those ancient piles rose huge and high
In rich irregularity;
Colossal form and figure fair
Seemed moving, breathing, living there.
The vaulted arch, where sunlight pure
Might never pierce the deep obscure,—
Where broadly barred, the ancient door
Was with such carving imaged o'er,—
The bending Gothic gable-roof
Of past magnificence gave proof;
The modern window's formal square
With Saxon arch was mingled there,
Whose stern recesses, dark and deep,
The figured iron stanchions keep.

BRUSSELS.

THE racking clouds were fleeting fast
Upon the bosom of the blast;

In wild confusion fiercely driven
Fled they across the face of heaven.
The fitful gust came shrieking high ;
The rattling rain flew driving by ;
But where the horizon stretched away
Towards the couch of parting day,
A streak of paly light was seen,
The heaped and darkling clouds between.
Against that light, for time full brief,
Brussels arose in dark relief.
Colossal on the western fire
Seemed massive tow'r and slender spire.
Nearer, and nearer as we drew,
More strongly marked the outlines grew,
Till of the buildings you might see
Distinct, the Gothic tracerie.
The drawbridge rung,—we passed the gate,
And regal Brussels entered straight.

It stirs, to see the human tide
That marks a city in its pride !
That fitful ocean's eddying sweep
Is still more changeful than the deep ·
For those dark billows as they roll
Mark movements of the human soul.
Yet in that city there was none
Of that confused and busy hum,
That tells of traffic and of trade ;
No, Brussels' time of power was sped :

Yet in her streets was something seen
Spoke what the city once had been.

Our rapid course as now we wheel
Where rose the huge Hôtel de ville,
The noble spire's proportions high
Stood forth upon the cloudy sky
In all its fretted majesty:
And his last light the sun had sent
On buttress and on battlement;
That, while the houses were arrayed
In all the depth of twilight shade,
Yet shot there, faint, a yellow glow
Where the tall arches shafted show;—
Glimmered a moment there the ray,
Then fainter grew, and past away.

Brussels, thy battlements have been
Of many an action strange the scene!
Thou saw'st, on July's dreadful night,
The veterans rushing to the fight:—
Thou heardest when the word was spoken;
At midnight thy repose was broken
By tramp of men and neigh of steed,—
Battalions bursting forth to bleed;
Till the dark phalanx' waving crest
Forth from thy gates was forward prest,
And breaking with the morning mild
The distant roar of battle wild.

And, later still, the rabble shout,
And revolution's riot rout;
Leaving such marks as long shall tell
Of dark destruction fierce and fell.

THE MEUSE.

THE sky was clear, the morn was gay
In promise of a cloudless day.
Fresh flew the breeze, with whose light wing
Aspen and oak were quivering:
From flow'ret dank it dashed the dew,—
The harebell bent its blossom blue,—
And from the Meuse the mist-wreaths grey
That morning breeze had swept away,
Showing such scenes as well might seem
The fairy vision of a dream.
For changing still, and still as fair
Rock, wave, and wood were mingled there;
Peak over peak, fantastic ever,
The lofty crags deep chasms sever:
And, grey and gaunt, their lichened head
Rose sheerly from the river's bed,
Whose mantling wave, in foamy sheet,
Their stern, projecting bases beat;
And, lashed to fury in his pride,
In circling whirlpools swept the tide,
As threatening, on some future day,
Those mighty rocks to tear away,—

What though their front should seem to be
A barrier, to eternity !
And on its side, the cliffs between,
Were mazy forests ever seen,
That the tall cliff's steep flanks so grey
Were clothed in mantle green and gay.
Long time along that dell so deep,
Beside the river's bed, we sweep ;
So steep the mighty crests inclined,
None other pathway you might find ;
Till the tall cliff's gigantic grace
To undulating hills gave place,
And vineyards clothe the bending brow,
'Stead of the clinging copsewood now.

COLOGNE.

THE noon was past, the sun was low,
Yet still we felt his arid glow ;
From the red sand, reflected glare
Deadened the breeze, and fired the air.
The open sky was misty grey ;
The clouds in mighty masses lay,
That, heaped on the horizon high,
Marked Alpine outlines on the sky.
Long had we toiled to gain a brow
On which we stood triumphant now,*

* [Two lines following are completely erased in the MS.]

While the white mist was certain sign
Where took his course the mighty Rhine.
Hills in the distant haze were seen,
And wide expanse of plain between,
Whose desert length, without a tree,
Was stretched in vast monotony.
We drove adown that hill amain ;
We past along the shadeless plain ;
Rested we now where, uncontrolled,
The Rhine his bursting billows rolled ;
And ever, ever fierce and free
Bore broadly onward to the sea.

ANDERNACH.

TWILIGHT'S mists are gathering grey
Round us on our winding way ;
Yet the mountain's purple crest
Reflects the glories of the west.
Rushing on with giant force
Rolls the Rhine his glorious course ;
Flashing, now, with flamy red,
O'er his jagg'd basaltic bed ;
Now, with current calm and wide
Sweeping round the mountain's side ;
Ever noble, proud, and free,
Flowing in his majesty.
Soon upon the evening skies
Andernach's grim ruins rise ;

Buttress, battlement and tower
Remnants hoar of Roman power,—
Monuments of Cæsar's sway,
Piecemeal mouldering away.
Lo, together loosely thrown
Sculptured head and lettered stone
Guardless now the archway keep
To rampart huge and frowning keep.
The empty moat is gay with flowers,
The night-wind whistles through the towers,
And, flapping in the silent air,
The owl and bat are tenants there.

EHRENBREITSTEIN.

OH ! warmly down the sunbeams fell
Along the broad and fierce Moselle ·
And on the distant mountain ridge,
And on the city and the bridge,
So beautiful that stood.
Tall tower and spire, and gloomy port
Were made and shattered in the sport
Of that impetuous flood,
That, on the one side, washed the wall
Of Gothic mansion fair and tall ;
And, on the other side, was seen,
Checked by broad meadows rich and green ;
And scattering spray that sparkling flew,

And fed the grass with constant dew.
With broader stream and mightier wrath,
The Rhine had chosen bolder path,
All yielding to his forceful will;
Through basalt gorge, and rock-ribbed hill,
Still flashed his deep right on.
It checked not at the battled pride,
Where Ehrenbreitstein walled his side;
Stretching across with giant stride,
The mighty waves the rock deride,
And on the crag, like armies, ride;
Flinging the white foam far and wide,
Upon the rough grey stone.
Beneath the brow of yon dark fell
Join the two brothers; the Moselle,
Greeting the Rhine in friendly guise,
To mingle with his current flies.
Together down the rivers go,
Resistless o'er their rocky foe,
As lovers, joining hand in hand;
Towards the west, beside their strand
They pass together playfully,
Like allied armies' mingled band:
Towards the east white whirls of sand
The torrent tosses by.

The morning came, and rosy light
Blushed on the bastions and the height,
Where traitor never stood;

While, far beneath in misty night,
The waters wheeled their sullen flight,
Till o'er them far, for many a rood,
The red sun scattered tinge of blood;
Then, broadening into brighter day,
On the rich plain the lustre lay;
And distant spire and village white
Confessed the kiss of dawn,
Amid the forests shining bright,
Still multiplying on the sight,
As sunnier grew the morn.
We climbed the crag, we scaled the ridge,
On Coblentz looked adown;
The tall red roofs, the long white bridge,
And on the eye-like frown
Of the portals of her palaces,
And on her people's busy press.
There never was a fairer town,
Between two rivers as it lay,
Whence morning mist was curling grey
On the plain's edge beside the hill.—
Oh! it was lying calm and still
In morning's chastened glow
The multitudes were thronging by,
But we were dizzily on high,
And we might not one murmur hear
Nor whisper tingling on the ear,
From the far depth below.

The bridge of boats, the bridge of boats—
Across the swift tide how it floats
In one dark bending line !
For other bridge were swept away ;—
Such shackle loveth not the play
Of the impetuous Rhine ;—
The feeble bridge that bends below
The tread of one weak man,—
It yet can stem the forceful flow,
Which nought unyielding can.
The bar of shingle stems the sea,
The granite cliffs are worn away ;
The bending reed can bear the blast,
When English oak were downward cast ;
The bridge of boats the Rhine can chain
Where strength of stone were all in vain.

Oh ! fast and faster on the stream
An island driveth down ;
The Schwartzwald pine hath shed its green
But not at Autumn's frown ;
A sharper winter stripped them there,—
The tall, straight trunks are bald and bare :—
The peasant, on some Alpine brow,
Hath cut the root and lopped the bough ;
The eagle heard the echoing fall,
And soared away to his high eyrie ;
The chamois gave his warning call,
And higher on the mountain tall

Pursued his way unweary.
They come, they come—the long pine floats !—
Unchain the bridge, throw loose the boats,
Lest, by the raft so rudely driven,
The iron bolts be burst and riven !
They come, they come, careering fast !—
The bridge is gained, the bridge is past,—
Before the flashing foam they flee,
Towards the ocean rapidly ;
There, firmly bound by builder's care,
The rage of wave and wind to dare,
Or burst of battle-shock to bear,
Upon the boundless sea.

ST. GOAR.

PAST a rock with frowning front,
Wrinkled by the tempest's brunt,
By the Rhine we downward bore
Upon the village of St. Goar.
Bosomed deep among the hills,
Here old Rhine his current stills ;
Loitering the banks between,
As if, enamoured of the scene,
He had forgot his onward way
For a live-long summer day.
Grim the crags through whose dark cleft,
Behind, he hath a passage reft ;

While, gaunt as gorge of hunted boar,
Dark yawns the foaming pass before,
Where the tormented waters rage,
Like demons in their Stygian cage;
In giddy eddies whirling round
With a sullen choking sound;
Or flinging far the scattering spray,
O'er the peaked rocks that bar his way.
—No marvel that the spell-bound Rhine,
Like giant overcome with wine,
Should *here* relax his angry frown,
And, soothed to slumber, lay him down
Amid the vine-clad banks that lave
Their tresses in his placid wave.

HEIDELBERG.

Now from the smiling afternoon
The rain had past away;
And glimmered forth the pallid moon,
Amid the heavens grey.
Brake, and bush, and mead, and flower
Were glistening with the sunny shower;
Where, from the tangled, viny wreath,
The clustered grape looked out beneath,
Climbing up the southern side
Of the round hills' bosom wide,—
Branches of the chain that bound

All the south horizon round.
Far towards the western day
Mannheim's towers softened lay.—
But a moment :—darkly down
Came the thunder, heaven's frown !
'Mong the trees, a fitful shaking
Told the hoarse night-wind was waking.
Grey upon his mountain throne,
Heidelberg his ruins lone
Reared colossally ;
All begirt with mighty trees,
Whistling with the even's breeze,
Flapping faintly by.

It was morning :—from the height
Cumbered with its ruins hoar,
All that lovely valley bright
We were looking o'er,
With its silver river bending,—
Vineyards to its banks descending.
Many a distant mountain chain
Girded round the mighty plain
Here the sky was clear and bright ;
But upon their distant height,
Like a monster o'er his prey,
Rain and tempest scowling lay ;
Like a mighty ocean-wave,
All along the horizon sweeping,
Flinging far its cloudy spray,

O'er the peaceful heaven beating.
But climbed the cloud yet more and more,
Into the heaven dancing,
Till,—like the scouring bands before
Embattled armies' path advancing,—
Circling the sun with mazy ring,
They wildly on came scattering.
Then deeper, darker, heavier grew
The fitful light the red sun threw
On the gaunt ruin's ghostly wall ;
And, coursing o'er the sloping meadow,
Strong was the light, and deep the shadow.
Till, rustling through the pine-trees tall,
Came quick the sound of raindrop-fall.
Fast increased, the leafy rattle
Spoke the coming tempest-battle.

Enter then the chambers cold—
Cold and lifeless, bald and bare ;
Though with banners decked of old,
Ivy tendrils' flickering flare
Are the only banners there.
Thou wouldst start to hear thy tread
Given back by echoes dead !
Thou wouldst look around to see
If a sprite were watching thee !
Yet a vision would come o'er thee
Of the scenes had past before thee ;—
Of the time when many a guest

Blessed the baron for his feast ;
When the peasant, homeward stealing,—
Dusky night the hills concealing—
Heard the swell of wassail wild,
Cadence from the castle coming,
Mingling with the night-breeze humming ;
And, until the morning mild
Lightened upon wall and tower,
Beacon-light from hour to hour
Streaming from the windows tall
Of the barons' ancient hall :
Where the shout around was ringing,
And the troubadour was singing
Ancient air and ancient rhyme—
Legend of the ancient time :—
Of some knight's blood, nobly spilt
In the melée or the tilt ;—
Of the deeds of some brave band,
Oath-bound in the Holy Land,
Such as iron Richard led,
Steeled without and steeled within,—
True in hand and heart and head,
Worthy foes of Saladin.
Or, if pleased, a darker theme ;—
Of spectres huge, at twilight seen
Above some battle-field,
Mimicking with motion dread
Past combat of those lying dead
Beneath their cloudy pinions spread—

Crested helm, and spear, and shield,
In the red cloud blazonèd.

Thus with feast and revelry
Oft the huge halls rang with glee;
All reckless of the withering woe
Reigned in their dungeons dank below,
Where, in the lone hours' sullen flight,
The masked day mingled with the night;
Until the captive's practised eye
Could pierce the thick obscurity—
Could see his fetters glance, or tell
The stones which walled his narrow cell:
Till, at the time the warder came,
His dusky lamp's half-smothered flame
Flashed on him like that sun whose ray,
And all the smile of lightsome day,
He has almost forgotten.

[THE BLACK FOREST.]

OH! the morn looked bright on hill and dale,
As we left the walls of merry [Kehl],
And tow'rd the long hill-ridges wound
That ramparted the plain around,—
That, greener growing as we neared,
At length with meadows decked appeared,
Fair as our fields in May; and then

We entered on a little glen,
Those miniature Alps among,
All smiling with a morning sun;
Grassy, and woody, and most sweet
As ever fairy her retreat
Formed for her midnight dances.   Through—
Tracing, in mazy winds anew,
The spots it had passed o'er, as fain
To run its sweet course o'er again,—
Flowed a small tributary stream
That the Rhine levied.   All between
The frontlets of the fair, fresh hills
Leaped merrily the glad, young rills,
Smiling in silver as they sprang,
And merry were the notes they sang:
For they were joyful at their birth
From the cold prisons of the earth
To the warm sun, and open sky;
And their song was all of liberty.
But the dell narrowed as we went;
Till, 'twixt the promontories pent
It upward ran; and the clear stream
Now forward shot, its banks between,
Fast flashing; till from the obscure
Emerged we on a lofty moor,
Open, and shelterless, and bare,
And gently undulating far;
With here and there a patch of pine
Breaking the smoothness of its line.

[ENTRANCE TO SCHAFFHAUSEN.]

THE eve was darkening, as we climbed
The summit of the hill ;
And, cradled 'mid the mountain-pine,
The wind was lying still.
Beneath the forests shadowy
Long time our path wound on ;
One narrow strip of starry sky
Between the dark firs shone.
The drowsy gnats had ceased their song,
The birds upon the boughs were sleeping,
And stealthily across our path
The leveret was leaping.

THE ALPS FROM SCHAFFHAUSEN.

" It was drawing towards sunset when we got up to some sort of garden promenade—west of the town, I believe ; and high above the Rhine, so as to command the open country across it to the south and west. At which open country of low undulation, far into blue,— gazing as at one of our own distances from Malvern of Worcester-shire, or Dorking of Kent,—suddenly—behold—beyond !

" There was no thought in any of us for a moment of their being clouds. They were clear as crystal, sharp on the pure horizon sky, and already tinged with rose by the sinking sun. Infinitely beyond all that we had ever thought or dreamed,—the seen walls of lost Eden could not have been more beautiful to us ; not more awful, round heaven, the walls of sacred Death." (*Præterita*, I. vi.)

SABBATH eve is sinking low
O'er the blue Rhine's sullen flow.

He has worn a prisoned way
'Neath the round hills' bending sway.
Far and near their sides you see
Gay with vivid greenery.
Many a branch and bough is bending
O'er the grey rocks, grim impending.
Danced the leaves on the bent twigs high,
Skeleton-like on the evening sky.
And the oaks threw wide their jaggèd spray
On their old, straight branches mossed and grey,
And the foam drove down on the water's hue
Like a wreath of snow on the sapphire's blue.
And a wreath of mist curled faint and far,
Where the cataract drove his dreadful war.
The Alps! the Alps!—it is no cloud
Wreathes the plain with its paly shroud!
The Alps! the Alps!—Full far away
The long successive ranges lay.
Their fixed solidity of size
Told that they were not of the skies.
For could that rosy line of light,
Of unimaginable height,—
The moony gleam, so far that threw
Its fixèd flash above the blue
Of the far hills and Rigi's crest
Yet russet from the flamy west,—
Were they not clouds, whose sudden change
Had bound them down, an icy range?—
Was not the wondrous battlement

A thing of the domy firmament?
Are they of heaven, are they of air?
Or can earth bring forth a thing so fair?
There's beauty in the sky-bound sea,
With its noble sweep of infinity:
There's beauty in the sun's last fire,
When he lighteth up his funeral pyre:
There is loveliness in the heaven's hue,
And there's beauty in the mountain's blue;
But look on the Alps by the sunset quiver
And think on the moment thenceforward for ever!

THE RHINE.

WE saw it where its billow swells
Beneath the ridge of Drachenfels;
We saw it where its ripples ride
'Neath Ehrenbreitstein's beetling pride;
We saw it where its whirlpools roar
Among the rocks of gaunt St. Goar—
In all its aspects 'tis as fair!
That aspect changes everywhere.
From Rhætian and Dinaric crest,
From the wild waters to the west,
From fearful Splügen's glaciered head,
The mighty torrent dashes, dread;
And, swelled by every Alpine snow,
Now see it chase these cliffs below,

On whose high summits deeply rent
Rise many a fortress battlement,
Seeming the lords of rock and hill,
And mighty in their ruin still.

VIA MALA.

OUR path is on the precipice!
How far, far down those waters hiss
That like an avalanche below
Whirl on a stream of foamy snow!
I've seen the Rhine when in his pride,
All unresisted, undefied,
Rolled smoothly on his aged tide.
I've seen the Rhine with younger wave
O'er every obstacle to rave.
I see the Rhine in his native wild
Is still a mighty mountain-child,—
How rocked upon his tortuous bed!
Came up, from the abyss of dread,
The deafening roar with softened sound,—
Murmuring up from the profound
Of distance dark, where light of day
Pierced not the thick, damp, twilight grey,
To the precipices sharp and sheer
Whence the white foam looked up so clear.
On looking o'er the barrier
From that rock-shelf, that hung so high

'Twixt the far depth and the blue sky,
Above, beside, around there stood
The difficult crags in order rude
Soaring to the thin, cold upper air,—
Looked forth unnaturally clear,
Jagged with many a piny spear.
And here and there a patch of snow
Contrasted strangely with the glow
Of the red, rough, mighty cliffs, and shed
A strange, cold light through the yawning dread
Of the abyssy gulph below.

SPLÜGEN.

A LITTLE cultivated space
Amid the rocky wilderness,—
It was not so conspicuous seen,
Where every mountain-top was green;
But that a little hamlet lay,
With its enclosures, 'mid the array
Of the dark pines, most peacefully:
And a few cattle strayed along,
Browsing the grass the rocks among,
Ringing their bells; and here and there,
Poised on rock-pinnacles i' the air,
Looked out from his round glassy eye
The mountain-goat suspiciously.
And, drop by drop, a little spring

Down the smooth crag came glistering,
With a sweet, tinkling sound, and fell
Into a mossed receptacle,—
The long trunk of an aged fir.
You scarce could see the water there,
So clear it ran, and sparkled round,
Then gurgled o'er the grassy ground,
Marking its course by the fresh green
Of the grass-blades it danced between.
I drank, and rested, and would fain
Have stopped to gaze, and gaze again,
And rest awhile the wearied eye,
Wearied with wild sublimity.
No! on! the peaceful bourne is past,
The rocks around are closing fast:
Higher and higher tow'rds the heaven
Betwixt the cliffs our road is riven;
Or twining round the hillside bare
With many a bend, where the high air
'Gan to blow cold, and damp, and keen,
But sharp, and pressureless.   The green,
Though fresh upon the mountain-side,
Was now more thinly scatterèd.
Now might you see, in sheltered nook,
The snow-arch o'er the icy brook,
With strange, white, delicate, bridgy curve
That the green light shot through above.
And round, beneath, beside, there grew
The Alpine rose's heathery hue,

That blushed along the mountain-head.
Was never flower so regal-red!
It climbed the scathed old rocks along,—
Looked out, the cold, white snow among,
And, where no other flower would blow,
There you might see the red rose grow.

THE SUMMIT.

OH, we are on the mountain-top!
The clouds float by in fleecy flock,
Heavy, and dank.   Around, below,
A wilderness of turf and snow,—
Scanty rock-turf, or marble bare,
Without a living thing; for there
Not a bird clove the thin, cold air
With labouring wing: the very goat
To such a height ascendeth not;
And if the cloud's thick drapery
Clove for a moment, you would see
The long, white snow-fields on each side
Clasping the mountain-breast, or heaped
In high, wreathed hills, whence torrents leaped,
And gathering force, as down they well
To aid the swift Rhine's headlong swell.
And here and there a mouldering cross
Of dark pine, matted o'er with moss,
Hung on the precipice, to tell

Where some benighted traveller fell ;
Or where the avalanche's leap
Hurled down, with its wild thunder-sweep,
Him unexpecting ; and to pray
The passing traveller to stay,
And, looking from the precipice
Dizzily down to the abyss,
To wing to heaven one short prayer,
One, for the soul that parted there.

CHIAVENNA.

OH, softly blew the mounting breeze
Through Chiavenna's myrtle trees,
And o'er the green hills' viny spread,
That rose in many a rounded head
Beneath the Alpine rocks of red.
And the fresh snow had fall'n that night,
And sprinkled with its mantle white
The mountain-amphitheatre
That rose around us far and near,
Though in such far confusion hurled
They looked to rule o'er all the world ;
And the white clouds seemed to immerse
Another ruined universe.

LAGO DI COMO.

"We took boat on the little recessed lake of Chiavenna, and rowed down the whole way of waters, passing another Sunday at Cadenabbia, and then, from villa to villa, across the lake, and across to Como, and so to Milan by Monza." (*Præterita,* I. vi.)

ALL along that quiet bay
A range of little shipping lay,
With their red flags drooped downward right,
And sheltered by their awnings white
From the high sun's red, scorching look,
That o'er the living waters shook
A blaze of hot and swarthy glow.
When we had launchèd from below
The shade of the tall cliffs, and came
Where Como rolled his breast of flame,
Down southward winding far away,
The olive's tints of gentle grey
Stooped to his borders, from between
The hills' uncultivated green.
And orange-groves him girded round,
Blossoming o'er him fragrantly ;
And in the sleep of his profound
White villages shone silently.
And from our prow the ripple's flash
Threw forth its little sparkles paly ;
The light sound of the oar [blades'] dash
Came dancing on the waters gaily.

There was blue above, and blue below,
And the gleam of the eternal snow.
And all along the shore, where'er
The storm-winds wont to chafe the wave,
The crucifix is shrinèd there;
That Christ may hear the passioned prayer
—May hear, may pity, and may save!

CADENABBIA.

OH! coolly came, on Como's lake,
The lovely beams of morning mild,
That o'er the Lecco mountains break,
And red their summits piled;
That, high above their olive shore
Their weary winter garments bore.
The broad boat lay along the tide;
The light waves lapped its sloping side,
And soft perfume of orange-trees
By fits came on the landward breeze.
The trouts shot through the waters blue,
Like small stars in the heaven glancing;
Or hid them where the broad weeds grew,
With wavy motion dancing.
Away, away, across the lake
How fast retires yon myrtle brake,
All sprinkled with a silver shower,
Through the dark leaves of lemon-flower.

Clear, as if near,—nor faint, though far,
Shines on the mountain, like a star,
The rock-born torrent's milky spray.
And many a small boat on its way
Urged by a breeze that bore them well,
Though unfelt as invisible,
With sunshine on their winglike sail
Past, like young eaglets on the gale.

The steps were broken, mossed, and steep ;
The waters sparkling, clear, and deep ;
The rock was high, the cavern dark,
Scarce lit up by the jewelled spark
Of the cold stream that under earth
Was, darkling, buried at its birth ;
Nor once its wave had sunned, nor seen
Aught but dark rock, and ice-caves green,
Where the dark waters, as a home,
Received the torrent's churnèd foam.
We launched again, and downward bore
A while beside the centre shore ;
Then left the shadowy eastern lake,—
Crossed through thick vines the wooded cape,
Struck the clear wave with long, light oar,—
Left a white wake that sought the shore ;
High o'er the boat the awning spread,
And, quick as sunned waves flashed before,
Toward the southward fled.

MILAN CATHEDRAL.

THE heat of summer day is sped ;
On far Mont Rose the sun is red ;
And mark you Milan's marble pile
Glow with the mellow rays awhile !
Lo, there relieved, his front so high
On the blue sky of Italy !
While higher still above him bear,
And slender in proportion fair,
Fretted with Gothic carving well,
Full many a spiry pinnacle ;
And dazzling bright as Rosa's crest,
Each with his sculptured statue prest,
They seem to stand in that thin air
As on a thread of gossamer.
You think the evening zephyr's play
Could sweep them from their post away,
And bear them on its sportful wing
As autumn leaves, wild scattering.

[LAGO MAGGIORE.]

IT was an eve of summer, mild
As ever looked the pale moon through,
That the deep waters were beguiled
Into such rest, that, as the blue,—
The moveless blue of the high heaven,—
Such sleep was to the low lake given

That, as in lethargy, it lay
Waveless and tideless, soft and grey
As chasmless glacier.   Voicelessly
The little barks came gliding by
Apparently without a wind,
Leaving long ripply wakes behind.
It would have seemed a lifeless sea,
But there arose colossally,
Beyond the mist-horizon, where
The waters mingled with the air,
The spirits of gigantic things,—
Lords of the earth, and air, and sky,
Where, while heaven's cloud around them flings
Concealment everlastingly,
The mountain-snow, like scattered flocks,
Speckled on high the red-ribbed rocks,
Or down the ravine's rolling blue
Its crisped surge o'er the green fields threw,
Flinging the ice-waves far and wide,
Like the tortured spray of the ocean-tide
Breaking broad on the mountain-side.
Yet was there such a softness shed
Upon the rude Alps' stormy head,
On massive wood and russet brake,
Flashing river and polished lake
So broadly stretched in sapphire sheet,—
Another heaven beneath our feet
Of deeper, darker, lovelier blue,—
It seemed that we were looking through

Those æther fields, so pure, so high,
Above the concave of the sky,
Where nor storm nor tempest cometh nigh,
And the moon she sits in her majesty.

GENOA.

Now rouse thee, ho! For Genoa straight!
We did not for the dawning wait;
The stars shone pale on Novi's gate,
And on the airy Apennine,
Whose towery steeps, with morn elate
Lay southward in a lengthened line.
And we knew,—and we knew,—and we knew
That from Elba to the Alps, o'er the broad sea's blue,
Where the wild waves wander and white ripples shine,
Looked the cloudy crest of the tall Apennine!
From the torrent's barren bed,
Bound by blocks of granite red,
Came the gay cicada's song;
Wheresoe'er the dew was dank
On the tree, the shrub, the bank,
All our scorching road along
Came the gay cicada's song.
While, beside our path, was seen
Of various trees a vista green,
Into the streamlet looking down,
Whose living crystal shot between,

All trembling with the leafy gleam.
And coolly on a high arch-span
The sportive light reflected ran
Hither and thither fast; and through
That natural-archèd avenue
There showed a rich and mighty plain,
Rolling its wooded waves away;
And, through the stretch of that champaign,
A noble river wound its way.
And on the horizon to the north
Pale gleams of icy sun came forth
From the St. Bernard's fastnesses;
White as the wreathèd salt sea-spray,
With the snow-wreaths that ever press
Upon that heaven-girt boundary,—
Boundary meet for Italy,—
Most meet for such a lovely clime,
As it looks o'er Marengo's sea
Unto the Apennine.
'Tis sweet, a topmost mountain-ridge
Impatiently to climb,
And there to stand, and dream away
A little space of time.
Oh! is there one remembers not
When first he saw the living deep,
With panting bosom, crimson-shot,
Call its smooth billows from their sleep,
That shout "the morn!" from steep to steep?
Whoe'er thou art, who hast not felt

Thou loved'st to be where sea-birds dwelt,—
To wander on the weary beach,
Just on the line the wild waves reach,
Or watch the petrels flit before
The marching tempest's warning roar,
And ocean-eagles dark and proud,
And white-winged ospreys skim the cloud ;—
And if thou ne'er hast felt as if
The ocean had a mind,
Nor held communion with the deep,
And converse with the wind,
When broad, black waves before it roll,—
I would not think thou had'st a soul.

PASSING THE ALPS.

To-DAY we pass the Alps,—to-day
High o'er the barrier winds our way,—
The barrier of boundless length !
The Queen of nations, in her strength,
Considered its recesses lone
Beseeming bulwark for her throne ;
Until her Carthaginian foe
Had soiled the yet unsullied snow,—
The eagle drove from her retreat,—
And woke the echoes from their sleep,
That ne'er had answerèd before
Save to the avalanche's roar.

Methinks upon the mountain-side
I see the billows of that tide,—
Of men and horses headlong driven
As clouds before the blast of heaven,
That ever change their hurrying form
In dark foreboding of the storm;
When the low sun's last light is shed
In glowing streaks of swarthy red;
And from his cave with fitful swell
Wakes the wild tempest's sounding shell.
So see the plumes, in dark array,
Roll on their yet untrodden way,
Unbroken yet with dreadful sweep!
Mark you that stormy, changeful deep?
Wave after wave is eddying on
And crested casque and morion
Flash frequent as the lightning flies
Among the armies of the skies.
But fiercer storm is gathering now
Than ever broke on Alpine brow;
And wild shall the confusion be,—
The strife of that tremendous sea
When, bursting from the Alpine chain,
It meets the storm on Cannæ's plain.

CHAMOUNI.

THE wreathing clouds are fleeting fast,
Deep shade upon the hills they cast,

While through their openings ever show
Enormous pyramids of snow;
Scarce can you tell in middle air
If cloud or mountain rises there,
Yet may you mark the glittering light
That glances from the glaciered height;
And you may mark the shades that sever
.The throne where winter sits for ever,
The avalanche's thunder rolling,
No summer heat his reign controlling;
The gloomy tyrant in his pride
Spreads his dominion far and wide,
Till, set with many an icy gem,
Rises his cliffy diadem.

Above a steepy crag we wound
Where gloomy pines his forehead crowned;
And heard we, with a sullen swell,
The turbid Arve dash through the dell;
You might have thought it, moaning by,
Wail for the loss of liberty;
For high the rocks whose mighty screen
Confined the narrow pass between,
And many a mass of granite grey
Opposed the torrent's forceful way;
So headlong rushed the lightning tide,
No pass was there for aught beside;
And we high o'er those cliffs so sheer
Must climb the mountain barrier,

Until unfolded to the eye
The fruitful fields of Chamouni.

It lay before us, as a child
Of beauty in the desert wild ;
Full strange it seemed that thing so fair,
So fairy-like, could harbour there ;
For fields of bending corn there grew
Close to the glacier's wintry blue ;
And saw we the same sun-ray shine
On pasture gay and mountain pine,
Whose dark and spiry forests rose
Till mingled with eternal snows
That climbed into the clear blue sky
In peaked, impending majesty.
'Tis passing strange that such a place
In all its native loveliness
Should, pent within those wilds so lone,
For many ages pass unknown—
Unknown save by a simple few
Who their own valley only knew,
Nor dared the mountain ridge that bound
That lovely vale with terrors round ;
That lived secluded from mankind,
Contented yet in heart and mind ;
That lived within that world alone,
A world of beauty of their own.
And now Helvetia's cliffy reign
Contains not in her Alpine chain,

In valley deep, on mountain high,
A race like those of Chamouni ;
For they have loved, at dawn of day,
To trace the chamois' fearful way,
Or on the toppling shelf of snow
With crags above and clouds below ;
Or on the peak whose spiry head
Is beetling o'er abysses dread,
Where place for foot, and grasp for hand,
Is all the hunter can command ;
Or on the glacier's rigid wave
Where he may find a chasmy grave ;
Returning with his spoils at even
Ere the red sun hath left the heaven.

[THE ARVE AT CHAMOUNI.]

I WOKE to hear the lullaby
Of the swift river rolling by,—-
Monotonous yet beautiful
Ever the gentle pebbly swell !
And every ripple lent his plash
Joining in chorus with the dash
Of every mighty mountain stream
That joyful sung his morning hymn,
His iris-glory round him quivering
Where his white showery falls were shivering.
There is a melancholy smile

On Nature's features fair the while,
When the dank dews descending grey
Weep for the loss of parting day ;
There is a sad and soft complaining
In the light breeze when day is waning ;
The evening star is fair and full,
But it is passing sorrowful ;
And merry is the laughing light
That blushes o'er the heaven's height,
That stream and bird and breeze and tree
For very joy sing merrily,
When wakes the morn the mountain snows
From their cold, fixed, pale repose.
It was a most enchanting vision !
The morning mists had upward risen
And, floating in the fields of air,
Lay in long lines most calmly there.
You could not call them clouds, I wist,
They were not smoke, they were not mist ;
They were a sort of visible breeze
Touching the tops of the pine-trees
That, as we passed beneath and strook
Their stretching branches, ever shook
The laughing showers of dancing dew
Reflecting every rainbow hue,
Or clinging to the clusters dank
Of bright green moss upon the bank.
And where those pines their crests had cloven
How rich the sun was interwoven !

And smiling through the leafy shade
Among the spangled grass it played,
And drank the dew from flower and blade,
Melting the heavy drops to air
That so dragged down the gossamer.

[EVENING AT CHAMOUNI.]

NOT such the night whose stormy might
Heroic Balmat braved,
When, darkening on the Goûté's height,
The tempest howled and raved.
Upon the mighty hill, forlorn,
He stood alone amid the storm ;
Watching the last day-gleams decay,—
Supposing its returning ray
Should see him lying there asleep,
With Alpine snow for winding-sheet.
Methinks I see him, as he stood
Upon the ridge of snow ;
The battering burst of winds above,—
The cloudy precipice below,—
Watching the dawn.   With proud delight
He saw that long, tempestuous night
Drive to the westward, and unfold
The ocean snow-fields, upward rolled,
Bright with the morning's glance of gold.
It past away,—the tossing flood

Of changing vapour, headlong riding;
And lo! the untrodden summit stood
Accessibly beside him.

[THE SOURCE OF THE ARVERON.]

THE foam-globes round come riding fast,
Like snow upon the eddies cast.
Forth from his cold and silent tomb,
Forth flies the river from the gloom.
The bars that echoed to his roaring—
Those icy bars have burst before him.
And now his chafèd surges see
Bound high in laughing liberty!
Oh, frigidly the glacier pale
Bears broadly to the nether vale!
Right in his cliffy, shivered side
Yawneth a chasm high and wide,
And from the portal arched and strong
Springs gladsome forth the Arveron.
Seems it an ancient forteresse,
All shattered in its mightiness;
The higher towers all rent and riven—
The battlements are downward driven—
And, that its form thou now couldst trace,
Froze to a mighty wilderness:
And that, its portal vast and old,
All archèd by the crisp ice cold,

And through whose chasms of paly green
The shivery sunshine shot between,
Or trembling with a meteor light,
Or dancing in the billows bright,
Smiling ethereally through
The ghost-lights of the crystal blue.

1834.

AT 15 YEARS OF AGE.

THE CRYSTAL-HUNTER (*May*).
THE INVENTION OF QUADRILLES [*Late in* 1834].
THE MONTHS (*December*).

THE CRYSTAL HUNTER.

[A FANTASY.]

I.

THE Crystal-hunter leaped aloft,—
Who shall climb so high as he
By the ribbed rock or the frozen sea?
And he hath past the avalanche,
New-fallen though it be.
The rock-moraine he heedeth not,
Nor torrent fierce and free;
Of these, and more, he bears the brunt;—
That granite wall upreared in front
To him no barrier must hold.
With morning strength, and bearing bold,
High on the mist-crag he must dare
A pathway in the middle air,
Where the white quartz with snowy streak
Marbles the frontlet of the peak.

II.

One effort more! He gains the top.
A moment on yon hanging rock

He stands to rest him, and to breathe,
Yet dares not cast his glance beneath ;
But fixed his eye, and nerved his limb,
To make the last decisive spring.

III.

A troubled glance the hunter threw ;—
" My limb hath scaled the Cervin,—Dru,—
Doth it here fail me ?   Rather may
The shivering granite fall away ! "
And he spoke truth.   The fearful ledge,
Projecting from its parent ridge,
Wavered beneath him.   One more roll ;—
Ave Maria, for his soul !
It hung a moment.   Nerve thee well !
It trembled, toppled, forward fell,
And bounded like a young gazelle
Into the air.   Six thousand feet
The roaring fragment down the steep
Dashed, like a meteor.   Once,—twice,—thrice,—
Loud crashed the echoes o'er the ice.
When the last thunder died away,
The hills seemed white with ocean spray.
An avalanche from every peak
Cut the pine-forests, fierce and fleet
As whetted scythe, and downward drew
A winter's snow upon the blue
Of the calm glacier, and the sound
Rang on the wild air-waves around.

IV.

And is he fallen? No! as yet
His foot is on the smooth crag set.
Yet wages he the awful strife
Sans fear of death, or hope of life.
Flashes his eye with bolder flame,—
He shakes the palsy from his frame,—
Springs from his rock-support unsure,—
And on the summit stands secure.

V.

In safety now, he cast his eye
Upon that spot of treachery.
Lo! whence the falling fragment flew
A cavern ran, the granite through,
Gloomy and vast; and from its sleep
Came sound of waters dark and deep,
Working a subterranean way.
The hunter hesitated not;
He dashed him headlong from the rock;
Lost at one plunge the light of day,
And through the darkness wound a way.

VI.

Lo! gleams of pale, phosphoric light
Flashed broad and wavy, clear and bright;
Red, purple, blue,—the pointed flame
From many a crystal cavern came.

Fretting the arched roof was seen
The speary, jet-black tourmaline;
'Mid the white amianthus' twist
Shone rose and purple amethyst;
And fresh the verdure, bright the green,
Where tree-like chlorite branched between.

VII.

"It is,—and yet it cannot be
The daylight in this cavern cold!"
Pierre advanced.   "It is! and see
The burnished sunbeam's glow of gold
Upon the floor of granite old!"
Yet a step farther; and behold
Such scene as has been dreamed of,—told,—
But never once believed to be !

VIII.

"Anzasca's vale is passing fair;—
Its châlets peaceful, meadows green;
And who has past his childhood there,
Beneath its heaven serene,
That will not think his valley-dwelling
Above all earth beside excelling?
Oh, would that I had never seen
The smiling of these pastures green,
Nor the snow-peaks that round them rise,—
These crystal streams, nor sapphire skies,—

Nor lived to see a fairer wild
Than that I played in, when a child!"

IX.

There reigned a magic silence there
Of rock and valley, earth and air.
No tinkling of the cattle-bell,
Nor song of shepherd on the fell.
The torrents waved and spoke; the breeze
Gave sound of life among the trees;
And one blue lake :—its gentle sweep
Owned, by the ripple on its deep,
All else was slumbering and sleep.

X.

The place had no inhabitant;
Nor through its coverts came
The step of any living thing.
It had nor memory nor name
Though a more heaven-like dwelling-place
Had never man's corrupted race.

XI.

There was a gathering of the Swiss,
When young Pierre had told his tale.
But clouds were on the mountain-brow,
And mist upon the vale.

And who shall dare the granite now
Amid the cloud to scale?

XII.

And still the silver hills put on
Their white and cloudy girth:
Impenetrably dark, the heaven
Stooped down upon the earth;
As if 'twould ne'er again be given
To man to see the birth
Of dawn upon the snowy hill,
Breaking broad and beautiful.

XIII.

Long time had past away before
The wild east wind awoke,
And rushing on the mountain top
The cloudy phalanx broke.
Then lustrously the ruby morn
Upon the châlets rose,
And gaily o'er the glacier
The crystal-hunter goes.
A hundred men they followed him,
As firm of foot as he;
And through the cleft and cavern cold
Past onward merrily.
And loud the shout that rang around
When opened to their view

The meadows by the icebergs bound,
The water's quiet blue;
And up and down the silver sound
Along the mountain flew.

XIV.

The meadows might have marvelled then
To see the châlets rise amain;
The woods might wonder, there to see
The people of the hill-countrie
Gathered together in a spot
Till then by mankind trodden not!
And now, who knows not Chamouni?
Is there an eye by which its fame
Hath never once been read?
Is there an eye to which its name
Hath not been blazonèd?
Yet this, the peopled wilderness,
The beautiful, the lone,
Was once a very dreary place,—
One of the mountain-fastnesses,—
Undreamed of, and unknown.

XV.

I think that nature meant it not
To be a celebrated spot:
That glacier blue, or cloudy rock,
Should be a sort of gazing-stock;

Or that her mountain-solitude
Be broken by intrusion rude.
Oh! I would dream, and sit, and see
The avalanches foaming free,
And watch the white and whirling cloud,
And hear the icebergs crashing loud;
And when the silver dawning shone,
Oh! I would climb a peak of snow,
And sit upon its topmost stone,
And see that I was all alone!

Before May 10.

[THE INVENTION OF QUADRILLES.]

ONCE on a time, the wight Stupidity
For his throne trembled,
When he discovered in the brains of men
Something like thoughts assembled.
And so he searched for a plausible plan—
One of validity,—
And racked his brains, if rack his brains he can
—None having, or a very few!
At last he hit upon a way
For putting to rout,
And driving out
From our dull clay
These same intruders new—
This Sense, these Thoughts, these Speculative ills.
What could he do?—He introduced quadrilles!

[*Late in* 1834.]

THE MONTHS.

I.

FROM your high dwellings in the realms of snow
   And cloud, where many an avalanche's fall
Is heard resounding from the mountain's brow,
   Come, ye cold winds! at January's call,
On whistling wings; and with white flakes bestrew
   The earth, till February's reign restore
The race of torrents to their wonted flow,
   Whose waves shall stand in silent ice no more;
But, lashed by March's maddened winds, shall roar
With voice of ire, and beat the rocks on every shore.

II.

Bow down your heads, ye flowers! in gentle guise,
   Before the dewy rain that April sheds,
Whose sun shines through her clouds with quick surprise,
   Shedding soft influences on your heads;
And wreathe ye round the rosy month that flies
   To scatter perfumes on the path of June:
Till July's sun upon the mountains rise
   Triumphant, and the wan and weary moon
Mingle her cold beams with the burning lume
That Sirius shoots through all the dreary midnight gloom.

III.

Rejoice! ye fields, rejoice! and wave with gold,
    When August round her precious gifts is flinging.
Lo! the crushed wain is slowly homeward rolled;
    The sunburnt reapers jocund lays are singing:
September's steps her juicy stores unfold,
    If the Spring blossoms have not blushed in vain:
October's foliage yellows with his cold:
    In rattling showers dark November's rain,
From every stormy cloud, descends amain,
Till keen December's snows close up the year again.

December.

1835.

AT 16 YEARS OF AGE.

JOURNAL OF A TOUR
THROUGH FRANCE TO CHAMOUNI, 1835.

"I determined that the events and sentiments of this journey should be described in a poetic diary in the style of Don Juan, artfully combined with that of Childe Harold. Two cantos of this work were indeed finished—carrying me across France to Chamouni —where I broke down, finding that I had exhausted on the Jura all the descriptive terms at my disposal, and that none were left for the Alps." (*Præterita*, I. viii.)

CANTO I.

1.

" Now, as you need not ride with whip and spur, I
  Beg very seriously to advise
That you should never travel in a hurry."
  Thus slowly spoke the doctor,* looking wise.
We took the hint, and stopped at Canterbury.
  Then in the morning early did we rise,

* "I had a sharp attack of pleurisy in the spring of '35, which gave me much gasping pain, and put me in some danger for three or four days, during which our old family physician, Dr. Walshman, and my mother, defended me against the wish of all the scientific people to have me bled. 'He wants all the blood he has in him to fight the illness,' said the old doctor, and brought me well through, weak enough, however, to claim a fortnight's nursing and petting afterwards." (*Præterita*, I. viii.)

But not to see the place where old Tom Becket is,
  Nor where the monks have heaped such heaps of
      bones—
I'm sure, enough to make any one sick it is—
  Under the old cathedral paving-stones,
Nor any other similar antiquities,
  Nor the museum, rich by gifts and loans :
But 'twas to trot to cliff-encircled Dover,
And think how we could get the carriage over.

2.

I'm sure enough to fluster anybody 'tis
  To step upon the stones of Calais quay ;
You meet with such a curious set of oddities ;
  This way and that you turn yourself to see,
And then you bawl out, " Dear ! how very hot it is ! "
  Then you're hauled off—for they make very free,
Those interfering officers of custom—
  For they will search, ay, and they will examine ;
—It's very impolite, but then, they must, ma'am !
  "They should not be so rough, and rout, and ram in
My things so ! "—But they're used to it ; only trust 'em ;
  You will make all things right by dint of cramming.
—Now, sir, I hope you've finished with that box ;
See, here's the key ; and that's the way it locks !

3.

There is a monument beneath the wall
  Of Calais, as you pass along the pier,—

A plain, unsculptured, low memorial ;
   Yet pass not by it, stranger ; for 'tis dear—
A thing most precious in the sight of all
   Who dwell upon the deep.   There lie not here
The bones of those whose names thereon you see ;
   But 'tis a tomb for such as have no tomb,—
Memory of those who have no memory,
   Nor even a burial-place, except the gloom
And ceaseless roll of the relentless sea ;
   For whom no hymn was sung except the boom
Of waves innumerable, and the roar
That their grave makes upon their native shore.

4.

Weep not for those who in their honours die,
   Whom fame forbids to perish,—for the brave !
The mighty and the glorious all pass by,
   All must go down into the voiceless grave.
Weep not for those for whom whole nations sigh,—
   But we will weep for those who died to save
The stranger perishing.   Approach and read !
   There's not a name upon yon simple stone
But of a hero.   What although the dead
   Have all gone down into the deep unknown,
And what although their bones be scatterèd
   All underneath the deep, salt surges thrown ?
They speak, for whom their being was surrendered :
They have been wept, and they shall be remembered.

5.

Then by Montreuil to Abbeville we went,—
    An ancient place, and picturesque indeed all ;
The ramparts round enclose a large extent.
    We put our noses into the cathedral
(Much tempted by the outside) with intent
    To wander through the nave inside, and see 't all ;
But started back, and instant sought the door,
    Nought seeing there but dirt and dirty people.
—The marble chequers of the ancient floor,
    Oh, citizens of Abbeville, why not sweep well ?
We stared about, the Gothic front before,
    Surveyed the porch, and criticised the steeple,
Marvelled to see the carving rich, and talked of
The figures standing with their noses knocked off.*

6.

And so we wandered on, until the Seine
    Glistened along the distance mistily,
Floating among the azure of the plain
    Like Milky Way along the midnight sky ;
Which wooded hills surrounded with a chain
    Of silver cliffs ; and Rouen's minster high,

* " In this journey of 1835 I first saw Rouen and Venice—Pisa not till 1840 ; nor could I understand the full power of any of those greater scenes till much later. But for Abbeville, which is the preface and interpretation of Rouen, I was ready on that 5th of June, and felt that here was entrance for me into immediately healthy labour and joy." (*Præterita*, I. ix.)

Uplifted in the air its Gothic flight
    In rich array of spiry pinnacle.
The river, that we looked on from the height
    Was full of islands green, and wooded well,
Like fairy dwellings in the misty light
    That o'er the city and the waters fell,
Throwing a beautifully golden shower
On minster grey and tall St. Ouen's fretted tower.

7.

Now, every street in Rouen without fail is
    Traversed by gutters of enormous size
(The joke about the Grecian quite stale is),
    But, in such occupation of your eyes
Beware lest you endure the fate of Thales
    —Ditched in philosophising on the skies.
For, as you pass each antiquated street
    Diverging from the Place de la Pucelle,
Over your head the Norman houses meet,
    Black with old beams, and ornamented well
With huge, broad roofs to shade them from the heat;
    And you enjoy variety of smell
Quite infinite,—in fact, you can't suppose
Better amusement for the eyes and nose !

8.

Rouen is full of holes and corners curious;
    What thing you are to see next, there's no knowing;

And churches two, applied to use injurious,
  Sounded with anvil-stroke and bellows blowing.
The rascally canaille !—it makes one furious !
  What English mob would ever think of stowing
Old iron 'neath the Gothic portals grey
  Of holy shrine, whose niches, statueless,
But carved and sculptured in a wondrous way,
  Remained to tell how sacred once the place ?
Indignant at the deed, we turned away
  Toward the huge Cathedral's western face.
I stood, upstaring at the lofty steeple
—And ran against a dozen market-people !

9.

It is a marvel, though the statues cramp are,
  How beautifully rich the tower is !
But 'tis amazing what a sudden damper
  Of all enthusiasm a shower is !
Down came a thunder-cloud, which made us scamper
  Under the arch that shows what hour it is.
—I don't admire the plan of elevating
  A clock upon a steeple huge and high,
Where really nobody can see it, bating
  Those who have got a very practised eye ;
And people in a hurry can't stand waiting
  Until the clappers tell how time goes by :
Besides, on Gothic work, the great, flat face
Looks quite incongruous, and out of place.

10

So, as the Rouen architects thought fit
  To go upon a plan entirely new,
They built an arch on purpose, every bit;
  Chiselled it over, till gay garlands grew
Beneath their hands, where'er their mallets hit,
  And open flowers along the granite blew
Unwitheringly.   On the arching wide
  Stood up the dial, bridging over quite
The narrow Norman street from side to side.
  Long distance down the street the dial white
By every passer-by might be espied,
  And looked exceeding picturesque and light.
In fact, there never was a plan projected
By which a clock could better be erected.

11.

So, as I said before, past this we ran
  (For, in this clime, when thunder-clouds come blowing,
Always retire as quickly as you can);
  Reached the hotel, and scarce had time to go in
Before the thunder and the rain began;
  So we sat at the window, and cried "Oh!" when
There came a brilliant flash along the sky.
  We, from the next day's morn till day departed,
Went up and down in Rouen constantly;
  Admired, and wondered that in every part it

Presented rich street-pictures to the eye.
And then we ordered horses, and we darted
Many a long look at beautiful St. Ouen,
Climbing a verdant hill, the last that looks on Rouen.*

12.

St. Germain is a pleasant place to mope at—
Uninteresting as a place may be.
There's a fine view 'twould be as well to stop at
Near the old palace; and they say you see,
Beyond, the spires of Paris; and I hope that
It's true, but it is only an "*on dit.*"
When you've walked up the Rue la Paix at Paris,
Been to the Louvre, and the Tuileries,
And to Versailles, although to go so far is
A thing not quite consistent with your ease,
And—but the mass of objects quite a bar is
To my describing what the traveller sees.
You who have ever been to Paris, know ·
And you who have not been to Paris,—go!

13.

By Soissons, and by Rheims,—which is much spoken of;
There's very little in it to admire,—
The statues' heads [indeed] are not all broken off,—
The thing is well preserved, from porch to spire;

* "Of Rouen, and its cathedral, my saying remains yet to be said, if days be given me, in ' Our Fathers have told us.' The sight of them, and following journey up the Seine to Paris, and then to Soissons and Rheims, determined the first centre and circle of future life-work." (*Præterita,* I. ix.)

And clean and neat, which is a [welcome] token of
   Good order here.   But many spires are higher :
The carving is not rich, the Gothic heavy ;
   The statues miserable,—not a fold
Of drapery well-disposed in all the bevy
   Of saints, and bishops, and archbishops old
That line the porches grey.   But in the nave I
   Stared at the windows, purple, blue, and gold :
And the perspective's wonderfully fine,
When you look down the long columnar line.*

14.

So on by Chalons, where no lions are
   Save four on the Hôtel de Ville, we past
Plains in abominable flatness far
   Extending westward, till we dropped at last
Down in a hole upon the town of Bar.
   I love to see a streamlet flashing past
Down some still valley, in a sportive mood ;
   Where the winds come to bathe themselves, and sing,
And dip their breezy tresses in the flood.
   'Tis sweet to stand and watch the quivering
Of wave-embarrassed beams, where pebbles strewed
   Brightly along the bottom of the spring

---

* " By the ' carving ' I meant the niche-work, which is indeed curi-
ously rude at Rheims; by the ' Gothic' the structure and mouldings
of arch, which I rightly call 'heavy' as compared with later French
types ; while the condemnation of the draperies meant that they were
not the least like those either of Rubens or Roubillac.   And ten years
had to pass over me before I knew better." (*Præterita*, II. vi.)

Fling, back and forward, flashes—constant play
Of silver sunbeams that have lost their way.

15.

Therefore we went along the river's bank
   Shaded by many a broad tree, branching wide
Where the cool ripple made the borders dank.
   And everywhere along the valley-side
The hill, upon its brown and sunburnt flank,
   Bore full and verdant vineyards in the pride
Of fruitfulness.   But though we hear a deal of
   Italian vineyards, and the juice delightful
Which Spanish peasantry make every meal of;
   And though a glass looks pretty when it's quite full
Of sparkling wine; and though we like the feel of
   A bunch of grapes just gathered with a slight pull;
And though the Grecian poets praised a foamer
Of wine, when they were thirsty (witness Homer);—

16.

Yet, sir, you would by no means think it fun,
   And all your fine romantic feelings fly off,
When you are stewed beneath a burning sun
   Panting with heat which you are like to die of,—
The stones beneath you scorching, every one,—
   The walls around you white and hot,—a sky of
Untempered, sultry, and continual blue,—
   The air without a motion or a sound;—

'Twould put a salamander in a stew
    To feel the dry reflection from the ground!
Vine, vine, still vine,—the only thing in view,—
    All vine, monotonously roasting round!
'Twould make you cry, as up the hills you scramble,
"Oh, for an English hedge of shady bramble!"

17.

From Bar-le-Duc we made a dash at Nancy,
    Whose beautiful arcades we walked about.
Its buildings are, as everybody can see,
    By revolutionists much knocked about.
There are two fountains spouting on a plan we
    Admired,—the triumphal arch is talked about.
But if you wish to see a foreign town,
    Look out for every narrow, dirty street,
As you walk diligently up and down;
    Pop into it directly; you will meet
Such combinations,—houses tumbling down,—
    Old fragments,—Gothic morsels, quite a treat,—
Columns and cloisters,—old *boutiques* which stink of
Garlic, and everything that you can think of!

18.

Long had I looked, and long I looked in vain
    For the pale mountains in the distance showing.
It was a hill that we had climbed: the plain
    Beneath lay brightly, beautifully glowing.

Is it a cloud, that yon pale, azure chain
    The whole, wide, low horizon round is throwing?
Oh no! the peaks are high on Jura's crest,—
    The plains do worship to their distant might,
The clouds by day couch, drowsy, on their breast,
    And the stars gleam along their flanks by night;
There comes the storm to dwell, the mist to rest;
    There, like commencing spirits, from their height
They echo at the thunderbolt's behest,
That gleams with lightning eye from east to west.

19.

We saw them all the way to Plombières,
    Which is a pretty place; but it is *not* that
Which makes the crowds of invalids go there.
    The springs are so abominably hot, that
They steam and bubble in the open air,
    Which makes the place look like a boiling pot, that
Smokes from the valley.   There the baths are seen,—
    The water, through distilling drop by drop there,
Fills from large tubs with liquid warm and green.
    There sit the social invalids and pop their
Thin yellow.noses out like lobsters lean
    Boiling for dinner.   Hour to hour they stop there,
Sleeping or reading,—subjects lean and bony,
Engaging in a conversazione.

20.

I'm on the Jura.   Lo! the rocks are dun,
    Although the opposite of heaven [is] bright,

And all the glare of gaudy day [is] done ;
   And there is shadow mingled with the light.
The dazzled world is weary of the sun ;
   Her eyes are shaded by the hand of night.
Yet beautiful, oh ! beautiful the beam
   Along the azure of the plain [is] sleeping :
The distant hills are veiled as with a dream
   Of mist, of dewy mist, their foreheads steeping.
The heaven is parting with the dying gleam,
   And lo ! the heaven is sad, the heaven is weeping.
The voice of streams is heard upon the hill ;
No murmur from the plain, and all the world is still.

21.

Farewell, ye plains ; ye champaigns wide, farewell !
   The cloud, the storm, the mountain now for me !
Mine be the deserts where the chamois dwell,
   And the wide eagle soars at liberty !
For Meditation on the pinnacle
   Of the lone mountain sits, and loves to see
The beauty of the living solitude ;
   And music floats around ; the mountain air
With a rich spirit of music is imbued ;
   And every sound becomes harmonious there ;
The streamlet's plash, the thunder of the flood,
   The flock's low tinkle o'er the pastures bare,
And the long roar and echo never-ending
Of distant avalanches, terrible, descending.

22.

So, on the heights of Jura, as I said,
  I stood, admiring much the setting sun
Taking a bath before he went to bed
  Out of the mists, that, indistinct and dun,
And dark, and grey, and colourless as lead
  Along the horizon's farthest outline run
Like velvet cushions for his weary head ;
  Or like a sort of scene, for him to slip off
Behind : and a long line of ruby red
  Zigzag'd along their summits, like a strip of
Dutch gold upon a piece of gingerbread
  After the happy urchin's gnawed the tip off
The finger, after long deliberation
Between his appetite and admiration.

23.

So, on the heights of Jura, as I said,
  I stood, and rocks around in quantities,—
In cliffs quite high enough to turn your head,
  And make you cry "How very grand it is !"
Especially after coming through the dead
  And stupid plains of France, where scant it is
Of beauty, and monotonously low.
  These are those famous rocks by which the stone-
Examiners have all been puzzled so.
  For here and there the granite blocks are strown

Over the bending mountain's softer brow;
   And some affirm that here they have been thrown
By mighty floods, quite large enough to heave a
Mountain across the valley of Geneva!

24.

When o'er the world the conquering deluge ran,
   Rolling its monster surges, far and wide,
O'er many an ancient mountain's lofty span,
   And when upon the all-devouring tide
Wallowed the bulk of the leviathan
   Where cultivated plains are now descried;
And when the toppling peaks of mountains old
   Were shook from their foundations into ruin,
Like shingle at the ocean's mercy rolled,
   That worked, and worked,—ever its work undoing,—
Heaping up hills beneath its bosom cold,
   Then wide again the devastation strewing,—
Then the dark waves, with nothing to obstruct 'em,
Carried these blocks from far, and here it chucked 'em!

25.

Such are the dreams of the geologist!
   He sees past ages of the world arise;
Strange sounds salute his ears, prepared to list,
   And wondrous sights, his rock-inspirèd eyes.
Before him solid mountains wave and twist,
   And forms of life within them fossilise;

The flint invades each member as it dies,
    And through the quivering corse on creeps the stone,
Till in the mountain's hardened heart it lies,
    In nature, rock,—in form, a skeleton ;
Much for the feature valued by the wise,
    Or in some huge museum to be shown,—
A mystery, as wonderful, at least,
As that of apples conjured into paste !

26

Thus on the Jura dreamed I, with nice touch
    Discriminating stones ; till, which was teasing,
The evening mists rolled round, with dampness such,
    That, though they brought a coolness not unpleasing,
They made me sneeze !   Now, nothing half so much
    Disturbs a person's sentiment as sneezing :
It takes you impudently by the nose ;
    Throws your component parts into confusion ;
And shakes you up, as doctors shake a dose
    In which they've put some villainous infusion ;
And the shrill echo in at both ears goes
    With such a sharp—[so] startling an intrusion
Like a fell thunder-clap by tempest brought,
Breaking the deep, still silence of your thought.

27.

And so I wished myself good luck, you know,
    As many people do on like occasion :—

The Swiss takes off his hat with a low bow
   To you, though in the midst of conversation ;
And if you've caught a little cold or so,
   You keep your friend just in the situation
Of the caparisoned dragoon, with sword on
   His side, well carved in wood, with wooden steed,
Placed the extremest limit of a board on :
   Still up and down he goes, by ball of lead
Which slowly swings beneath him, ever spurred on :—
   Thus at each sneeze your friend still bows his head ;
In fact, the courteous Swiss puts off and on his
Hat, like a master of the ceremonies.

28.

A mountain walk by moonlight, people say,
   Is interesting and poetical.
Some like to walk while twilight wastes away ,
   Some choose to be Peripatetic all
Night, and a very Stoic during day.
 · I am not given to be ecstatical
When I can't see, and therefore I descended ;
   Although the night that came was scarcely night,—
So softly with the air was starlight blended,
   Like the sea's phosphor lustre, coldly bright ;
The peaks above me, as I downward wended,
   Grew misty in the ray so faint and white ;
You could have thought, as, veil-like, you did view them,
That the moonbeams were shining through and through
     them.

29.

Then did we leave Poligny, and to Morez
    We went, which is an odd place in a hole,
Under huge cliffs built in successive stories
    Of limestone, very pretty on the whole,
Swiss-ish, and picturesque, and so on : nor is
    It far from the green summit of the Dôle
Which groves of tall and spiry pine embrace,
    [And], like a mantle of the deepest green,
Shadow its sides and darken round its base :
    But grassily doth rise its crest ; between
Its ridges and in every sheltered place
    The wavy lines of whitest snow are seen :
Through the first summer months it wears them yet,
Like a large emerald in silver set.

30.

Reader, if you are trigonome——, no ! I
    Can't manage that long word, which is a bother ;—
Trigonometrical, I'll tell you how high
    It is above the Medi——, there's another !—
Mediterranean ; and that will show why
    The snow, although it melts some time or other,
Continues there so long. I've calculated
    It is [five] thousand and [five] hundred feet
Above the sea. A summit, insulated
    So high, is seldom subject to much heat ;

And therefore, as above I have related,
   Although the sun's rays may appear to beat
Warmly upon the grass with towering glow,
They cannot melt the hard heart of the snow.

31.

And when the day is hot, at two o'clock,
   And trees and flowers are loaded with the heat,
And walnuts tall give shelter to the flock
   That cowers beneath their branches, then 'tis sweet
To seek the shadow of some lofty rock
   With a cool streamlet gurgling at your feet ·
And when you've scaped the power and the might
   Of the fierce sun, and coolness fills your breast,
Then, to look up to some enormous height
   Where winter sits for ever, and whose crest
Is lovely with the kisses of the light,—
   The ruby light that loves on it to rest,
And to feel breezes o'er your features blown, is
Like eating raspberry ices at Tortoni's !

32.

The meadows of these hills are like the robe,
   Bedight with gems, of some high emperor :
There's not a spot in all this lovely globe
   That's more abundant in its flowery store.
The Alpine rose along its ridges glowed,
   The mountains burning with the fiery flower.

Queen of the blossoms in the fields below,
  The silver lily lifted its pale head,
The emulation of the mountain-snow.
  Fresh emerald moss along the rocks was spread,
And harebells trembling as the breezes blow,
  And many another flower, of blue and red,
Purple and gold, "too numerous to mention,"
Half-drowned in dew, "solicited attention."

33.

—Attention difficult to give, when we
  Saw such a scene of loveliness around ;
Yet 'twas not much amiss to stoop, and see
  The beauty of that flower-enamelled ground :
First, to behold the mountain's majesty,
  Then, the fresh green of yonder mossy mound.
As when you enter some enormous pile—
  Gothic cathedral very ancient,
First, you admire what people call the style
  And massive wholeness of the monument,—
Magnificent effect of dome and aisle ·
  And next, you view the lavish ornament
That's carved on every part, but all intended
To make the general effect more splendid.

34.

Thus on the Jura did we gaze, beholding
  A monument enormous everywhere

The hills, that on their shoulders seemed upholding
    The high blue dome that looked above the air ;
Groves of dark pines their scarped crags enfolding ;
    Rocks raised like castles from their summits bare,
In many a varied form : and then did look
    At the most rich and intricate detail ;
The coloured marks in yonder marble rock,—
    The green moss that hangs o'er it like a veil,—
The turf inlaid with flowers,—the crystal brook
    That ever tells its never varied tale
Unto the air, that sporteth with its spray,
And sings, and sings, and sings to it all day.

35.

Give me a broken rock, a little moss,
    A barberry-tree with fixèd branches clinging,—
A stream that clearly at its bottom shows
    The polished pebbles with its ripples ringing ;—
These to be placed at Nature's sweet dispose,
    And decked with grass and flowers of her bringing ;—
And I would ask no more ; for I would dream
    Of greater things associated with these,—
Would see a mighty river in my stream,
    And, in my rock, a mountain clothed with trees.
For Nature's work is lovely to be seen ;
    Her finished part as finished whole will please ;
And this should be a mountain-scene to me—
My broken rock, my stream, and barberry-tree.

36.

I'm going to turn a corner,—which I've done
   A hundred or a thousand times before '
But this is really a distinguished one,
   And needs a little preparation, for
The shock of it is quite enough to stun
   You, like a box upon the ear, and floor
Your very feelings, that you will not move
   A muscle of your body, nor will dare
To breathe the breezes that about you rove.
   You could chastise the movement of the air
While drinking in the beauty that you love !
   Some cannot that delicious rapture share ;
Those who feel little, talk, and rant, and vapour,
Kick up their heels, prance, frisk, curvet and caper.

37.

Mighty Mont Blanc, thou hast been with me still
   Wherever I have been !   In the dark night
I've walked upon thy visionary hill,
   And have been filled with infinite delight :
And when I woke, it was against my will.
   Though then I did not have thee in my sight,
Still wert thou like a guiding star, and all
   My hope was to be with thee once again,
Hearing thy avalanches' fearful fall.
   I was bound to thee by a pleasant chain,

And I am here in answer to thy call !
  I see thee rise o'er yonder lordly plain,
Like nothing else i' the world ; for thou hast stood
Unrivalled still, thine own similitude !

38.

Nobly the hills are set on Leman's shore,
  Like to a dark and most tempestuous deep
Petrified into mountains ; and the power
  Of silence on the lake laid it asleep
In the arms of the mountains, evermore
  Embracing it.   Down, down the torrents leap
Into the calm waters, with a rush immense,
  Like headlong passion which appeased is straight
When it is met by gentle patience.
  And on the other side, in purple state
The plains spread out their broad magnificence,
  And gorgeously enrobed, and all elate
With corn, and vine, and forests deeply green :—
It was a lovely sight and beauteous to be seen !

39.

Now down the hill we heard our carriage roll,
  In our enthusiasm sent away.
—Enthusiasm is a parasol
  When the sun's hot ; and on a rainy day
As [an] umbrella doth the rain control :—
  A carriage, on a long and weary way,—

A cloak when it is cold,—a fan in heat,—
      Patience when you are out of patience.—Oh !
Down the hillside with still delaying feet
      How merrily and lightly did we go !
Although the sun did fiercely on us beat,
      And though it was some seven miles or so,
Our hearts were merry, and our limbs elastic,
Only because we were enthusiastic !

40.

Thus we went down the Jura, and before
      Our road had led us a long way past Gex, it
Showed us the villa, beautiful no more,
      —Voltaire's,—and the low, humble chapel next it,
With this inscription placed above the door
      Conspicuous, *Deo Voltaire erexit,*—
Which reads a little oddish !   This we past ;
      The hills increasing, nearer as we drew,
Till fair Geneva raised its spires at last,
      Sitting beside the waters bright and blue,
On which, though trembling with the noontide blast,
      Mont Blanc from far his silver image threw ;
And, nearer us, the waters did receive a
Clear image of the city of Geneva.

41.

Geneva is a rather curious town,
      And few its public edifices are.   How

The streets upon each side come sloping down,
　　Too steep for carriages, and rather narrow.
It has two bridges o'er the double Rhone,
　　Which darts beneath as swiftly as an arrow :
Forth from the lake it comes, with swirl and sweep,
　　Fed by the distant glaciers on high—
The reservoirs that hang on every steep—
　　And giddily the billows dance you by.
Thirty or forty feet the stream is deep ;
　　Strong as a giant ; azure as the sky ;
And clear and swift as a tempestuous wind they go,
And very like a painter's pot of indigo.

42.

Many a philosopher has scratched his pate,
　　Pronouncing it incomprehensible,
While standing on that bridge, and looking at
　　The waters passing by with ceaseless swell,
So richly, so intensely azure, that
　　You could imagine,—ay, and very well,
That heaven, 'neath the sun's excessive ray,
　　Was melting !   All the pebbles may be counted
Thirty feet down, it is so clear ; some say
　　That even from the river's icy fount it
Preserves its azure colour all the way.
　　—By this, the circumstance is not accounted
For,—that *green* (like the sea-green beard of Neptune).
Is nothing but an optical deception.

43.

In fact, it cannot be accounted for ;
   And nothing on the subject can be said !
There is no reason for it, any more
   Than that a cherry should be white or red,
Or a plum blue.   On all Lake Leman's shore
   The waves beat bluely, save just at its head,
Where the Rhone rushes from its glacier-fountains,
   It is a little turbid : that's no matter,—
Only a little granite from the mountains,
   Which torrents wear and tear, and lightnings shatter.
The river is soon cleared, nor far around stains
   The purity of Leman's crystal water.
I'd say 'twas like a sapphire,—but I've more
Than once used that similitude before !

44.

The scenery about Geneva's rich.
   On one side is the Jura, blue and bare ;
Opposite, is a valley, out of which
   From huge Mont Blanc and tall Argentière
Rushes the Arve, as dirty as a ditch.
   And if you ask for it, they'll take you where
The river, in romantic situation
   Between high banks of gravel, gushes down,
By its most foul "evil communication"
   Corrupting the "good manners" of the Rhone,

Which holds aloof from all the perturbation
   Of its foul neighbour, and goes down alone.
Some time it so continues: long it can't,—
Which I could moralise upon, but shan't.

45.

And in this valley which I have just spoken of
   Appears Mont Blanc, with silver summits three,
Whose wavy, domelike outlines finish, broken off
   Into aiguilles, which by his side you see
Splintered, and crushed, and rent,—a direful token of
   Ancient convulsions of their majesty.
There is Jorasse, Midi, and spiry Dru,
   And the Géant, and high Argentière:
And dark and scowlingly they look at you.
   There's not a spot of vegetation there—
Even where the hand of winter cannot strew
   Snows on the sides, so splintered and so bare,
With granite points upon their rugged flanks,
Like spears of the archangels' military ranks.

46.

But on your left a softer scene appears,
   Where the lake spreads out its metallic glow.
No mountain there its craggy outline rears,
   But all is peaceful,—beautifully so!
Some little bark in distance fades, or nears
   With forkèd canvas flitting to and fro

Over the dimples of its polished face.
Many a field and many a garden gay
Bedeck the Voirons' gently sloping base ;
At these you look and wonder, day by day,
So that Geneva is a pleasant place
Wherein to make a week's or fortnight's stay,
To rest and to enjoy yourself at ; and to
End a long journey, and a tiresome canto.

CANTO II.

WE left Geneva.   'Tis "against the grain"
From such a lovely place yourself to sever,
Knowing that you will not be there again
For a long time at least,—and perhaps never.
I must confess I crossed the bridge with pain,
The bridge that arches o'er the rushing river.
But up my heart leaped with a bound once more
When, full in front, increasing as we went,
The ancient mountain stood, with glaciers hoar.
And entering the valley, which is rent
Between the Môle and Brezon (I before
Have spoken of it), I grew quite content,
And ceased to sigh, though I no more could see of
Geneva's spires, which there are two or three of.

2.

Our road fast brings us nearer to the Môle,
  And we shall pass beneath it presently.
The Môle—now don't confuse it with the Dôle,—
  There is a difference between M and D—
The Môle, I say, sir, is upon the whole
  A lovely mountain as you'd wish to see.
Those who for height alone inclined to stickle are
  May say that it is nothing of a height;
"[Six] thousand feet, or something, perpendicular:
  That's quite contemptible!"—and they are right!
But I myself am not at all particular,
  So that a mountain's aspect please the sight;
And even to look up so high makes one feel
Stiff in the neck, from such a place as Bonneville.

3.

And on the other side appears the Brezon,
  A lofty precipice of limestone hoar.
Monsieur Saussure, who used to lay much stress on
  Necessity of practising, before
You venture into danger (and with reason),
  Used to climb up, and poke his numskull o'er
Couched on his breast,—a ticklish situation
  For those who are not thorough mountain-bred!
Oh, Shakespeare! when the paltry elevation
  Of Dover's promontory filled thy head

With dizziness and instant inspiration,—

    Oh, Master Shakespeare, what would'st thou have said

If, 'stead of poor four hundred, as at Dover,

Thou hadst lookt down four thousand feet, and over?

4.

Tell me of crows and choughs,—a pretty thing!

    Why, man, you could not see a flying cow

A quarter down!—or samphire-gatherer swing,—

    Such nonsense!—here were room and height enow

To hang a dozen of 'em in a string,

    Nor see the topmost from the mountain's brow.

"Not leap upright for all beneath the moon?"

    —No, nor leap backward from the verge of fear

For all beneath the shine of stars or sun.

    "Not hear the sea?"* why, here you could not hear

The echo of the chamois-hunter's gun

    Fired at the bottom of the cliff so sheer!

The valleys lying in the mountain's lap

Look like a pretty little pocket-map!

5.

Onward we went; and as we went, the cloud

    Fretted the sunny sky with silver white,

---

* *Edgar.* Hark! do you hear the sea?
Gloucester. No, truly.
  Edgar. The crows and choughs, that wing the midway air
        Show scarce so gross as beetles. Half-way down
        Hangs one that gathers samphire,—dreadful trade!
        You are now within a foot of the extreme verge;
        For all beneath the moon I would not leap
        Upright.   (*King Lear,* IV. v.)

Like Gothic carving on a temple proud;
    Pale at the first, and shadowy, and light;
Then darker and distincter, like a shroud
    Stooped upon each surrounding wintry height.
For these, where'er in heaven the clouds are lost,
    Do gather them together, and wrap over
Their naked sides, all comfortless with frost.
    Above us, wreathed like smoke the cloudy cover,
And half-way down the higher hills were lost;
    But here and there by chance you might discover
A spire of ice, incredibly on high,
Start like a meteor through the misty sky.

6.

Onward we went, in—what's the name of it?—I
    Really don't know if it has any name,
The vale 'twixt Cluse and Bonneville, which looks pretty
    At summer's early glow; though at the same
Time it is liable—which is a pity—
    To the attacks of water, wind, and flame.
You ask, at its wild beauty wondering,
    How can the place be such a *flat* as to
Permit the Arve its turbid wave to fling
    Over its greenest fields, and to renew
An annual devastation? till some king *
    (A monument's built to him) passing through
Bonneville (just at the bridge-end mark you it?)
"Aggeribus haec flumina coercuit."

            * [Charles Felix of Sardinia.]

7.

But when the fierce and unrelenting heat
  Of summer doth oppress the weary stream,
Along the hills the rays, all burning, beat,
  And the hot valley pants beneath the beam.
The glowing soil beneath you fires your feet
  And tires your eyesight with an arid gleam.
Once,—'twas a marvellous and fearful thing,—
  The trees took fire beneath the glowing soil ;
Wide Conflagration spread his purple wing :
  Vainly the frighted peasants pant and toil,
Vainly dig channels for the crystal spring ;—
  The helpless waters in their channel [boil],
And a red Autumn in an instant came,
And Nature withered 'neath her glance of flame.

8.

But when, in furry robe of whitest snow,
  The Winter spreads her desolate dominion
Forth come the winds, and loudly do they blow,
  And, like an eagle poised on threatening pinion,
Swoop in wide circles round the plain below.
  And when a tempest once begins within one
Of these low mountain-valleys, many a tree
  That long firm-rooted in their earth has stood
Bows his old head before it painfully ;
  And all the plain, obscured with hoary wood,

Undulates like the variable sea :
  The very river backward rolls his flood,
Shakes the far mountains with his echoing roar,—
Heaves his white crest on high, and deluges his shore.

9.

And now the bridge of Cluse is gained and past :
  Sharp turns the road to enter the ravine
Cloven in the hills as by some weapon vast.
  The river takes his rushing path between ;—
I would not be the Arve, to fly so fast
  Through the variety of such a scene !
From side to side, from crag to crag rebounding,
  Sheeted with foam, as is the spurred war-horse,
So leaps the river, that the rocks [surrounding]
  Are formed and chiselled by his constant force.
With bursting echoes quake the cliffs resounding,
  No deepness stills, no barrier checks his course ;
On, ever on, the maddened billows sweep,—
Rest in no pool, nor by their border sleep.

10.

The castellated cliffs stand o'er your head
  Broken, as is the war-worn battlement.
But, as if its defenders were not fled,
  Bristle the pines above their summits rent
Like a well-ordered army.   Bare and red
  Gleam their high flanks, and beautifully blent

Are moss, and turf, and crag, wet with the spray
 Of yon aërial stream, which long ago
We saw in distance glittering down, and gay
 With its broad, beautiful, perpetual bow
Belted about its column, as the ray
 Shoots through the dissipated drops below,
Like dew descending, or soft April showers
Bathing in sunshine the delighted flowers.*

11.

Oh, gently sinks the eve, and red [doth] set
 The sun above Sallenche's mountains blue;
Like regal robes, the purple clouds beset
 Mont Blanc; but on his crest, still breaking thr
The last bright western rays are lingering yet,
 And the white snow glows with a rosy hue.
And now it fades, and now is past away;
 The highest dome among the stars is white;
It seems to wake, and watch the night [decay]
 And kindle at the first gleam of the light,—
A mighty beacon, to proclaim the day,
 A beacon fit to meet the gladdened sight
Of half the world, from Gallia's plains of vine
Unto the distant ridge of the blue Apennine.

12.

The morning came; delightful was the weather.
 Up to the door with rattling rumble daundered

* [The Nant d'Arpenaz].

Those very strange compounds of wood and leather :—
   Oh, *char-à-banc*, thou vehicle most honoured
Of all the vehicles e'er put together !
   What though thy cushions be to sit upon hard,
And though they scarce can hold their well-squeezed
      three,
   And though thou lookest ancient, worn and brown,
What coach and chariot can compete with thee
   That knead the mud of Pall-Mall up and down,
Or traverse and re-traverse constantly
   The loud monotony of London-town,
With gilded panels, arms upon the door,
Footmen behind and coachmen cocked before ?

13.

I love to see, with stately gait advancing,
   The City coach, that vehicle historical,
With golden glare the vulgar eyes entrancing !
   I love to see the darting gig or curricle,
With pawing greys and harness brightly glancing !
   I love to see, with swiftness meteorical,
The mail-coach spurn the dust like clouds behind,—
   Eyes watching for it, expectation strung,
When "Troo, taroo, taraw !" comes on the wind !
   I love to see a chariot float along
On softest springs for luxury designed,
   Yieldingly firm, and delicately strong,—
With whirling wheel divide the lagging air,—
Steeds pant, dogs bark, boys shout, and rustics stare !

14.

But thou, of all to me the sweetest sight,
   Made for the mountain, servant of the hill,
Contemner of bad roads, who tak'st delight
   In crushing rock and stone, be with me still,
Friend of my wearied limb! For visions bright
   Rise on me when I see thee; by the rill,
The river, and the precipice I've past
   Safely and most delightfully in thee!
—Thus thought I, while around me progressed fast
   Bustling and packing:—"Where could that thing be?
And where could this have got to?"—till at last
   The things must be tied on, and steadily
Some twenty minutes were at last allotted
Ere the last cord was stretched, and tightly knotted.

15.

For the interior—how we could pack into
   So small a space so many things, I can't tell:
Baskets, and covered things that bore one's back into;
   Boxes and bundles,—everything one can't well
Want, or may possibly require: twines cracking, too,
   Things tumbling down because they cannot stand
      well:—
And "Tie that there," and then, "Tie that thing to it,
   And tie this on the top of them; and that thing
Must go between your legs;—ay, so you'll do it;—
   And this behind your back, it is a flat thing;

This on your knee."—No, thank ye ; I'll give you it !—
  "This in your pocket."—How that bottle's rattling !
"Dear me, it's loose ; how lucky you have spoken !"
  Smash ! "That's the tumbler ; hope it is not broken !"

16.

We'd sixteen miles to go, or thereabout.
  That, among hills, is something appetising.
Hadst seen us, you'd have said, I make no doubt,
  Our provend-preparation was surprising :
With lemonade (you cannot get brown stout,
  The creamy bubbles through its crystal rising),
Bottles of wine and brandy, butter, bread,
  Cheese of the finest,—cream and rich Gruyère ;
Strawberry jam upon our crusts to spread,
  And many a purple plum, and golden pear,
And polished apples, blushing rosy red ;
  Ham, beef, and bacon, slices rich and rare ;—
We found our knives and dishes useful ; you
On carrying them may find them useful too.

17.

Thus from St. Martin's gate we made a start, I
  Following in the second *char-à-banc.*
Behind us in a third there came a party
  Who, dashing down for Italy point-blank,
Here from their route had ventured to depart ; we
  Found them agreeable, and free, and frank.

The day was very hot, and quite a smotherer,
　　That makes one drowsy, which is very odd.
Some of us, who inclined to make a pother were,
　　Quite disturbed those who were inclined to nod
By playing at bopeep with those in t'other *char,*—
　　Popping behind the leathern curtains broad.
I was ashamed, and told them—"no more gammon
Think that a shocking way of going to Chamouni!"

18.

There is a little and a quiet lake,
　　And lovely are its waters, hardly seen,
Lying beneath the shelter of a brake,
　　Like the spring turf beneath its foliage green ;
And where the sunbeams through the leavage break
　　They dive beneath its waters, with a sheen
Such as the moon sheds on the midnight deep,
　　When mermaids, issuing from their coral caves,
With shelly voices sing the seas to sleep,
　　And scatter wayward lustre o'er the waves.
Forth the stream issues with a hurried leap
　　Down its rock-girded channel, which it paves
With many a ball of alabaster white,
And marble gay, and crystal clear and bright :—

19.

Not clearer than its waters, which receive
　　The image of Mont Blanc upon their breast,

Nor, with the motion of one ripple, heave
    The quiet snow on his reversèd crest,—
So beautiful the scene, you might believe
    A limner, 'mid the fairies deemed the best,
Had painted it with natural colours fair,
    And put the water o'er it for a glass,
And framed it in, with fretwork rich and rare
    Of jewel-flowers, and moss, and daisied grass.
How sweetly sounds the gurgle through the air
    Of the cool, dancing streamlet, as you pass :
There is no music pleases you so truly
As gush of waters in the heat of July.

20.

By slow degrees and winding pathway mounting,
    Onward we went the ancient pines among ;
By many a trickling stream and gushing fountain
    O'er the rough bed of many a torrent strong,
Amid the wreck of Servoz' ruined mountain *
    So beautiful in ruins.   Far along,

---

* [" L'aiguille de la Dérochée ou Dérotzia, à côté du col de ce nom. C'est de là que partit en 1751 le gigantesque éboulement, qui fit croire aux gens de la vallée de Servoz que la fin du monde approchait. D'autres, plus instruits, crurent qu'il s'était ouvert un volcan dans cette localité, et le savant Donati fut envoyé de Turin pour l'examiner, à ce que raconte de Saussure, *Voyages*, § 493. Des eboulements plus ou moins grands ne sont pas très-rares dans ces montagnes ; ce fut l'un d'eux qui, en 1837, combla le petit lac de Chède, l'un des plus jolis endroits de la route de Genève à Chamonix." (Alphonse Favre, *Recherches*, II. § 418.) The landslip of stanza 20 is therefore that which happened in 1751 ; and the lake, described in stanzas 18 and 19, was destroyed by another landslip only two years after Mr. Ruskin's visit.]

And up the ridge, amid whose granites grey
    Struggles the Arve, you hear the constant cry
Of waters, though unseen they wind their way
    A hundred fathom down.   In front, on high
The glacier flashes in the noontide ray,
    In the deep azure of the Alpine sky.
And now the ridge is won : rest, rest, and see
What lies beneath you now ; for there is Chamouni !

21.

Like the Elysian fields where rove the blest,
    Though round them reaches the Tartarean wild,—
Thus lies the enchanted vale, and all that's best
    Of Spring and Summer's lavished on their child.
While, round the space where those green meadows rest,
    Is mountain-chaos, like a barrier, piled,
And Winter holds an undisputed reign ;
    The chilly-fingered tempest-winds that go
On waving wings along the hills amain
    Shake not a blossom in the fields below ;
And every sunbeam that, with effort vain,
    Strikes on the cold and unrelenting snow,
Seeks the sweet covert of the sheltered plain
And lies delighted upon flowers again.

22.

The King of mountains, clothed in cloudy veil,
    Asserts his rule upon the meadows green,

And lays his sceptre on the subject dale—
　　Sceptre of silver ice, whose spires were seen
And many a minaret of crystal pale
　　Rising above the pines with silver sheen.
Oh, beautiful, how beautiful to see
　　The summer sun on tower and bastion beaming,—
Their bases beaten by a frozen sea,—
　　The moveless foam upon its breakers gleaming;
And from a mighty portal constantly
　　A sparkling river through the valley streaming;
For here's the "company" of glaciers, that is
"Supplying" all the world with water, *gratis!*

23.

Then we descended, through the valley going,
　　Till the small village in the front was seen
With its low spire conspicuously glowing,
　　(For here they cover all their spires with tin,
Which makes them sparkle in the distance, showing
　　Like diamond in gentleman's breast-pin).
Here there are several hotels; but which of them
　　May be the best, is difficult to say.
Accommodation may be found at each of them;
　　But don't believe those fellows on the way,—
They'll recommend the worst, if you trust speech of them '
　　The "Union" seems the largest and most gay;
Of which I'll give you an exact description,
Because it was the place of our reception.

24.

The " Union " is a building large and strong,
  And somewhat English ; and its sides are graced
With triple row of windows broad and long ;
  But at its end are wooden galleries placed,
Well carved and ornamented all along :—
  The Swiss in such things have a deal of taste.
And there the guides assemble, when the sun
  Is red upon the mountain's topmost snow,
And all the labours of the day are done,
  To smoke a sociable pipe or so,
Telling their feats of peril, one by one ;
  And happiest he who oftenest below
His foot hath trod that crest where none can stand
Save in a shadow of death, his life laid in his hand.

25.

In the interior are lobbies three
  Above each other, windows at each end,
From which—I will not tell you what you see
  At present,—in a minute I intend
To take the panorama properly.
  And in these passages I'd recommend
A walk for exercise in rainy weather,—
  They are so long, they're quite a promenade.
I've tramped away in them for hours together,
  And measured miles before I dreamed I had.

And in them there are pictures which are rather
    Well executed, or at least not bad,
Of ibex, deer, and chamois, bisons, buffaloes,
Which those who hunt 'em say are rather tough fellows.

26.

From this the bedrooms open, clean and neat,
    Well furnished ; and which often furnish you
With much amusement.   It is quite a treat
    When you have nothing in the world to do,
Close to the window oped to take your seat,
    And feast upon the magic of the view.
I went to one ; 'twas at the lobby-end,
    Full opening on the gigantic hill,
Up went the casement : there I took my stand,
    Stupidly of the scene to take my fill :
My head dropped somehow down upon my hand
    Sleep-like ; and I became exceeding still.
Sometimes, when such a glory you espy,
The body seems to sleep,—the soul goes to the eye.

27.

The noonday clouds across the heaven were rolled
    With many a lengthened vista opening through
Where many a gorgeous wave of white and gold
        [*No more was written.*]

[A LETTER FROM ABROAD.]

DEAR RICHARD,*

AT Paris, in the Rue la Paix,
Last Midsummer I sit reviewing ·
And think of you, now far away,
And wonder what you may be doing :—
If after church at school you stay,
Not yet come back from Wales ;
Or if at Herne Hill glad and gay,
Returned from Doctor Dale's.
I love to write to you, and so,
Our journey hither well digesting
I write, altho' I hardly know
What may be chiefly interesting.

---

* "Some six or seven gates down the bill, a pretty lawn, shaded by a low-spreading cedar, opened before an extremely neat and carefully kept house, where lived two people, modest in their ways as my father and mother themselves,—Mr. and Mrs. Fall. Their son, Richard, was a year younger than I, but already at school at Shrewsbury.
Richard Fall was entirely good-humoured, sensible, and practical ; but had no particular tastes ; a distaste, if anything, for *my* styles both of art and poetry. . . . We got gradually accustomed to be together, and far on into life were glad when any chance brought us together again." (*Præterita*, I. viii.)

You'll guess the time went very slow
When I was being closed and stewed up,*
But then there was a pretty go
When I escaped from being mewed up !
The day was fine as day might be ;
We cantered down to Canterbury ;
Then on to Dover ; crossed the sea ;
Stopped, as we were not in a hurry,
At Calais ; walked about to see
The Gothic steeple, and the people :
I sketched, in manner bold and free,
A sketch at which you'll like to peep well.
Next morn was thick and dark with rain ;
But on the next we braved the weather.
Thinks I, "Oh, this is just the same,—
Their harness is as bad as ever !
Their horses still, in tail and mane,
Uncombed, unornamented brutes ! "
But soon I saw, and saw with pain,
There was a falling off in boots !
And so to Rouen on we went,
By many a hill full gay and green ;
The evening was magnificent ;—
The noble city, like a queen,
Sat in silence on the Seine
That here and there about was bent,

* [During the illness and convalescence described in the note on p. 181.]

With islands bright his waves between,
Like an emerald ornament.

HOSPICE OF GREAT ST. BERNARD: *July* 21.
9000 *ft. above sea.*

And there I sketched me sketches three,
Though Mr. Prout has nearly spent all!
Two of his pictures you may see
In the Annual Continental.
Up to Paris next we went all,
Seeing many an English face ;—
No wonder that they there are bent all!
'Tis a wondrous pleasant place.
On we went, enjoying rarely
Soissons, Rheims, and Bar, and Nancy,
—'Tis quite an itinerary ;—
We saw all that people *can* see.
But nothing pleased so much my fancy
As when we went to Plombières ;
—Far as the quickest eye could scan, we
Saw the Jura, blue and bare.
And now the sun is shining bright
On many a lofty crag of grey ;
And sheets of deep snow, silver white,
Beating back the flashing ray.
Mont Velan in his white array
Looks o'er the little lake of blue,
Whose verdant waves transparent play
With ice and blue snow shining thro'.

SCHAFFHAUSEN, 5 *August.*

The afternoon was clear and fair ;
The sun shot warm along the snow ;
The clearness of the mountain air
Like crystal gleamed, above, below.
And nearer drew the Velan's glow ;
While on the mountain-side were seen
Mosses most rich, of emerald green,
Sprinkled o'er with fairy show
Of Alpine flowers ; you cannot think
How sapphire-like the gentian blue
Mixed with stars of paly pink !
How humbly, and how low they grew
On every shadowy spot !
And I did think of home and you,
When from beneath a rock I drew
A young *forget-me-not.*
The dogs all out,—ay, every snout,—
Upon the snow they romped and rolled ;
How they pulled each other about !
How the young did plague the old !
They can't bear heat, as we were told,
But love to feel the constant cold.
They welcome you, altho' they're mute,—
There's such a manner in the brute !

Aosta ! oh, how thick it is
With buildings, ancient, strange and rare :

—I know you like antiquities ;—
Full twelve feet thick of brick laid bare,
The ancient city-walls are there,
With a marble ornament
By the chisel sculptured fair.
Broadly are the arches bent;
Tho', as the facings are defaced,
The old inscription is replaced.
It runs in French, to this intent :—
"Stranger, respect this monument!
Augustus Cæsar in the space
Of three short twelvemonths built this place,
And called it by his name.   Pass on!"
An arch of most triumphal span
Is there, of brick as hard as stone,
With this inscription thereupon
—I give it you as best I can :—
"Rome, in many a weary fight
O'er the Salassians victorious,*
Built this arch, remembrance glorious
And memorial of her might."
Much were we pleased, you may be sure,
When we set off for Cormayeur ;—
Fortresses arising round ;
Rocks, with ruined castles crowned ·
Vineyards green with trellised rail ;
Villages in every vale :
Alps on high of granite grey

* *Anno urbis* 724.

(Snow on every point appearing),
That, capped with cloud, seem far away,
Or vision-like, in heaven clearing.
Oh, the wild and worn array
Of the huge aiguilles you see
Waiting on the majesty
Of their monarch !   Oh, the gleam
Of his silver diadem !
With a thousand glaciers set
In his summer coronet
All the mountain's brow, they span it,
Barred about with spires of granite.
Avalanches, one and all,
Down they fall in what they call
—'Tis a sort of lonely valley
Full of ice—which they call " Allée
Blanche," but *blanche* it an't at all !
Mont Blanc is lifted up on high
And shakes his snowy head into it ;
Broken ice and granite strew it,—
'Tis confusion constantly.

TOP OF RIGI.

I hope all this is entertaining !
I think, if lesson-time's gone by
And play-time's come, and it is raining,
It may be so, at Shrewsbury.
But if the sun is shining bright,
And games agog, when you receive it

Then fold it up,—say "That's all right,"
And take your cricket-bat, and leave it.
When you're knocked up, and wickets down,
And when you panting, tired, and worn are,
Then in the school-room pray sit down
In that comfortable corner.
Then will you read, while you repose,
All that I am going to tell you,
Nor think the letter is verbose,
Nor say that I'm a tiresome fellow.
From Cormayeur we backward bore,
O'er St. Bernard's Alps again,
Down upon Lake Leman's shore
Where blue waves on Chillon roar.
Round by Neufchâtel we came,
By ancient Granson's towers of fame;
And where the Rhine for evermore
'Mid columnar rocks of grey
Thunders down with lightning spray,
Underneath an iris bright,
That arches o'er with trembling light.
'Tis sweet to see the peaceful thing
Around the warring waters cling,
With a sort of fearful quivering!
Then to Zurich, where I grew sick,—
Almost thought I should have stayed a
Day on purpose, but we made a
Dash at Zug, and heard fine music
Played by landlord and landlady.

Mont St. Gothard next we drew nigh,
By Altorf and the Lake of Uri.
The Swiss, as you know very well,
Are very fond of William Tell:
To show they've not forgot him,
A chapel's built where from the prow
Of Gessler's boat he leapt ashore,
And *ditto* where he shot him.
Up we went wondrous high
In the midst of the beautiful dark-blue sky,
'Mid St. Gothard's granites tall.
Down we went,—'twas fair and fine,
Down by zigzags twenty-nine,
Built upon the top of a wall
Close by a torrent's flashing fall.

HOSPICE OF THE GRIMSEL, 6000 *feet high.*
25 August,—a terrible day.

I wonder much what sort of day
This 25th of August may be
In dear old England far away!
Perhaps the sun is shining gaily,
And you may see, by Severn's stream,
The city basking in the beam,
And sloping fields with harvest white,
And distant mountains, bluely bright.
Now turn your gladdened eyes away
From all this landscape warmly gay;

And read, and think, and try to see
The scene that August brings to me.
I see around me, far and wide,
A weary waste of mountain-side,
Strewed with blocks of granite bare,
With scanty grass-blades here and there.
Above, the summits tall and proud
Are buried in a veil of cloud ;
But through the misty mantle show
The frosty fields of new-fall'n snow.
Thick and constant everywhere
The snow-flakes ride the rolling air.
The mountain-torrents loudly call
And fret the crags with constant fall.
The river that receives them all
Lifts up his voice on high
On, onward still, with constant gush,
The foam-flakes on his billows rush
Monotonously by.
The fire is bright ; the window-pane
Is thick with mist, and wet with rain.
My corner-seat, quite warm and cosy,
Makes me feel talkative and prosy.
So, where was I ?   Can't tell at all,—
So long and tiresomely I've pottered !
Oh yes, descending the St. Gothard,—
"Close by a torrent's flashing fall."
The interest of that pass to me
Lay in its mineralogy.

For that you do not care a fig.   I
Will take you to the top of Rigi.

The vapours came with constant crowd ;
The hill was wrapt up in the cloud.
Hour after hour 'twas misty still,
As evening darkened on the hill.
Before the sun had left the sky
The wind stretched out his mighty hand,
And back recoiled the clouds, and nigh
Out looked the sunset luridly,
Like smoulder of a dying brand ;
And white-edged thunder-clouds around
Gave forth a hollow, groaning sound.
Then onward came the cloudy tide ;
Again it met from either side ;
And darkness came, and darkness dire,
But cleft by constant sheets of fire.
Broad blazed the lightning's blinding flash,
With following thunder's instant crash :—
A pleasant night on which to be
Five thousand feet above the sea !
At half-past three we first looked out ;
The stars were sprinkled all about ;
The sky was blue, the air was clear,
And the white moon looked wondrous near.
The golden streaks of breaking dawn
Across the smiling east were drawn.
Relieved against the brilliant light

Dark purple outlines met the sight;
Which, brighter still as grew the flame,
Darker and purpler still became.
Round all the south, eternal snows
On dark horizon palely rose;
And it was beautiful to see
The light increasing constantly,
To search the gloom in valleys deep,
And wake the flowers on mead and steep.
Come, stand upon the Kulm with me!
The sun is up; on what shines he?
Mountain on mountain rosy red
With glacier helmet lifts his head.
Oh, the long chain of snow-fields white,
Like the pale moon of summer night,
Peak over peak with wondrous glow!
While wreathing vapours brew below;
And on the other side were seen
Innumerable champaigns green.
Far, and more far, and faint they grew,
Expansive, beautiful, and blue!
Many a large lake beneath us set,
Without a breeze its waves to fret,
Like silver mirror distant lay
In many a lovely creek and bay;
Reflected, sank beneath its strand
Dark woods and flowery meadow-land.
And, farther down, the mountains high,
And underneath, the morning sky.

The glittering towers of fair Lucerne.
City, and hill, and waving wood,
Blue glaciers cold, and sparkling flood,—
All that was marvellous or fair
Seen at a single glance was there.

THUN, 2 *September.*

I sit me down to make a whole
Of this long-winded rigmarole :
To put in order its confusion,
And bring the tale to a conclusion.
I've written it at different stations,
From very different elevations.
By writing as the journey goes on,
My dates are wondrously well chosen.
You see I've taken in its turn all ;
In fact, I've kept a sort of journal ;
Hoping it may be in my power
To interest a leisure hour,
And make your fancy cross the sea,
And roam in Switzerland with me.

VENICE.

THE moon looks down with her benignant eyes
   On the blue Apennine's exulting steep;
Many a large star is trembling in the skies
   Lifting its glory from the distant deep.
How high the marble-carvèd rocks arise,
   Like to a lovely thought in dreamy sleep!
Along the weedy step and washen door
   The green and drowsy surges, moving slow,
Dash on the ancient, tesselated floor;
   Or still, and deep, and clear, and coldly flow
Beside their columned banks and sculptured shore;
   Or waken a low wailing, as in woe,
Where sleeps beneath the unbetraying water
The victim, unrevenged, of secret midnight slaughter.

The palaces shine palely through the dark,
   Venice is like a monument, a tomb.
Dead voices sound along the sea; and hark,
   Methinks, the distant battle's fitful boom!
Along the moonlit pavement of St. Mark
   The restless dead seem flitting through the gloom.
There, melancholy, walks,—the Doge's crown

High on his gleaming hair,—the warrior grey.
How passionless a chill has settled down
   Upon the senator's brow !   A fiery ray
Gleams underneath the bravo's stormy frown '
   Who long ago have vanishèd, awake,
Now start together from the various grave,—
Live in the silent night, and walk the conscious wave.

[*Autumn.*]

SALZBURG.

On Salza's quiet tide the westering sun
Gleams mildly; and the lengthening shadows dun,
Chequered with ruddy streaks from spire and roof,
Begin to weave fair twilight's mystic woof,
Till the dim tissue, like a gorgeous veil,
Wraps the proud city, in her beauty pale.
A minute since, and in the rosy light
Dome, casement, spire, were glowing warm and bright;
A minute since, St. Rupert's stately shrine,
Rich with the spoils of many a Harzwald mine,*
Flung back the golden glow; now, broad and vast,
The shadows from yon ancient fortress cast,
Like the dark grasp of some barbaric power,
Their leaden empire stretch o'er roof and tower.

Sweet is the twilight hour by Salza's strand,
Though no Arcadian visions grace the land:
Wakes not a sound that floats not sweetly by,
While day's last beams upon the landscape die;

* The dome of the Cathedral of St. Rupert is covered with copper;
and there are many altars and shrines in the interior, constructed of
different sorts of marble, brought from quarries in the vicinity. St.
Rupert, to whom the Cathedral is dedicated, was by birth a Scotch-
man.

Low chants the fisher where the waters pour,
And murmuring voices melt along the shore;
The plash of waves comes softly from the side
Of passing barge slow gliding o'er the tide;
And there are sounds from city, field, and hill,
Shore, forest, flood; yet mellow all and still.

But change we now the scene, ere night descend,
And through St. Rupert's massive portal wend.
Full many a shrine, bedeckt with sculpture quaint
Of steel-clad knight and legendary saint;
Full many an altar, where the incense-cloud
Rose with the pealing anthem, deep and loud;
And pavements worn before each marble fane
By knees devout—(ah! bent not all in vain!)
There greet the gaze; with statues, richly wrought,
And noble paintings, from Ausonia brought,—
Planned by those master-minds whose memory stands
The grace, the glory, of their native lands.
As the hard granite, 'midst some softer stone,
Starts from the mass, unbuttressed and alone,
And proudly rears its iron strength for aye,
While crumbling crags around it melt away;
So midst the ruins of long eras gone,
Creative Genius holds his silent throne,—
While lesser lights grow dim,—august, sublime,
Gigantic looming o'er the gulfs of Time!

[*Autumn ?.*]

THE AVALANCHE.

The accident to which these lines allude occurred in the ye
Several guides, with Dr. Hamel, a Russian, and an Eng
were ascending the Mont Blanc; when they had crossed t
of ice above the Glacier of Bossons, an avalanche descend
the Calotte of Mont Blanc, which swept away several of th
two of whom were irrecoverably lost.

I.

THEY went away at break of day,
And brave hearts were about them,
Who led them on, but at the grey
Of eve returned without them.

II.

They're watched from yonder lowly spot
By many an anxious eye;
Hearts that forebode they know not what,
And fear, they know not why.

III.

"Why left ye, lone upon the steep,
My child?" the widow said:—
"We cannot speak to those who sleep;
We dwell not with the dead."

IV.

"Why comes not with you from the hill
My husband?" said the bride:—
Alas! his limbs are cold and still
Upon the mountain-side.

V.

His boy, in undefinèd fright,
Stood shivering at her knee;
"The wind is cold, the moon is white,
Where can my father be?"

VI.

That night, through mourning Chamouni,
Shone many a midnight beam;
And grieving voices wander by
The murmur of the stream.

VII.

They come not yet, they come not yet!
The snows are deep above them,
Deep, very deep; they cannot meet
The kiss of those who love them.

VIII.

Ye avalanches, roar not loud
Upon the dreary hill:
Ye snows, spread light their mountain shroud;
Ye tempests, peace, be still!

IX.

For there are those who cannot **weep**,
Who cannot smile,—who will not slee
Lest, through the midnight's lonely gl
The dead should rift their mountain-tc
With haggard look and fearful air,
To come and ask a sepulchre.

* This is a superstition very prevalent among the

[*Late in the year.*]

THE EMIGRATION OF THE SPRITES.

THERE was a time, in Anglo-land,
When goblin grim and fairy fair,
On earth, in water, and in air,
Held undisturbed command.
Ye hills and groves! lament, in grief—
Lament, and say, woe worth the day,
When innovating disbelief
First drove the friendly sprites away;
Then was there not a forest leaf
Without attendant elfin grey,
That sat to make the leaflet shake,
Whene'er the breezes chose to wake.

II.

There was not, then, a forest lawn
Where fairy ringlet was not made,
Before, through the surrounding shade,
The slanting sun bespoke the dawn.
There was no knoll beneath an oak
Where was not found, bestrewed around,

By woodman's child (from slumber woke
By singing birds' delightful sound)
Pink tops, from mushroom tables broke,
And acorn cups upon the ground,
From which so fine, when fairies dine,
They always drink their dewy wine.

III.

There was no fell on misty mountain,
Beneath whose darkling cliffs, at night,
There brooded not some shadowy sprite:
There was no swiftly flowing fountain
Without a spirit to preside;
And, on the moor, and by the fen,
The kelpie by the water-side,
(The bane of all wayfaring men)
Shook his bright torch, a faithless guide;
The brownie wandered in the glen,
Or stalked upon the hill-top high,
Gigantic on the evening sky.

IV.

The shepherd, in an ecstasy,
Unearthly voices seemed to hear;
Prophetic forms perceived, with fear,
To pass before his dreaming eye:
Perhaps beheld, at close of day,
With melancholy air beside him,
Those who, he knew, were far away:

Or long procession slowly gliding,
Or voice of battle's bursting bray,
Or troops upon the mountain riding;
And started back, and feared to see
A visible futurity.

V.

It was upon a starry night,
When winds were calm, and all around still,
The world of spirits called a council,
And every incorporeal wight
Came there his brother ghosts to greet :—
Some shoot, like falling stars, through heaven;
Some, like the Northern meteors, meet;
Some ride the clouds by tempests driven;
Some yoke the lightning's blazing sheet
By which the mountain-tops are riven;
Some came veilèd in vapours well,
Some voiceless and invisible.

VI.

A fairy, from the crowd advancing,
First in the conclave silence broke;
"Because these mortals" (thus he spoke)
"Are far too blind to see us dancing,
They think, forsooth! we never do.
Because we're of æthereal kind,
Formed out of mist and fed with dew,
Invisible as summer wind,

The blundering, earth-polluted crew
All faith in us have quite resigned.
Fairies (if we could cross the sea)
Are more revered in Germany."

VII.

He spoke : the fairies sitting round
Cried "hear !"   Along the voice did pass,
And shook the dew upon the grass ;
And the gnat hummed in with the sound.
A brownie next arose and spoke
(A Bodsbeck resident of yore),
Uncouth his form and stern his look,
And thus inveighed he : "Now no more
For me, behind the chimney-nook,
The bowl of milk stands creaming o'er ;
No more upon the board I see
Some dainty morsel left for me.

VIII.

"A certain shepherd, wont by night
To watch his flocks on Ettrick braes,
And who has sung a hundred lays,
Inspired by every mountain sprite,—
Who well my old achievements knew,
Began to tell some pranks that I did ;
But, when his tale was half-way through,
Paused in the story undecided,

Fearing that few would think it true,
And that the public would deride it.
He stopped, for fear of jest or banter,
And changed me to a Covenanter."

IX.

With waving plume of rushing flame,
A kelpie, leaping from his seat,
Thus to the council spoke · "Is't meet
That now no more the kelpie's name
Is named on any moorland stream?
These mortals say, and think they're wise,
That my existence is a dream;
And call my fickle fire, that flies
O'er every fen with brilliant beam,
Gases that from the waters rise;
And now, because such stuff gets credit,
I'm never followed, seldom dreaded."

X.

A travelled goblin next arose;
In foreign countries had been he,
Who thus addressed the company:
"Where Rhine beneath his castle's flows,
Full many a fairy train I met;
Dancing beneath some ruined tower
Upon a basalt summit set;
Or singing in a blossomed bower,

Or swinging in a spider's net ;
And many a ghost, at evening hour ;—
The peasants (an unpolished race)
Reverence the spirits of the place.

XI.

"So let us flit to yonder strand ;
Indeed you'll find it more amusing
Than to hear English boors abusing
The spirits of their native land."
Then from his seat each goblin bounded,
And each his mode of carriage chose ;
Wide murmurs through the forest sounded,
When th' incorporeal conclave rose.
Some whipped away, with speed unbounded,
In the red leaflets of the rose ;
And some chose bats and gnats to fly on,
Or mounted down of dandelion.

XII.

And, when they came where rolled the Rhine,
Whose mountain scenery much delighted them,
The native fairies all invited them,
On top of Drachenfels to dine.
And when the stars rode magnified
Above the steeples of Cologne,
And light along the river-side
From every cottage window shone ;

They hovered o'er the gloomy tide,
Or sate upon the topmost stone
Of some old Roman tower, and there
Still do they haunt the mountain air.

XIII.

Deserted England! now no more
Inspiring spirits haunt thy hills;
Nor spiritual being fills
Thy mountain æther as of yore.
No more shall fancy find its food
In torrent's song or tempest's roar;
Or hear a voice in solitude,
On hill and dale, by sea or shore.
No more shall Scotland's peasant rude
Recount his legendary lore;
The soul of Poesie is fled,
And Fancy's sacred fire is dead.

[*About Christmas.*]

[THE INVASION OF THE AL

THE forest boughs and leaves are still;
No sound disturbs the drowsy air;
Save upon yon crag-buttressed hill;—
A motley crowd is gathered there,
The young, the fearless, and the fair;
And the old man with gleaming hair.
And there is lifting of hands in prayer:
For the foe down their valley his army hath le
Village and hamlet in ruin are red:
Like a plague, through the night they passe
      leaving only
The desolate hearth, and the hall very lonely.

[*About December.*]

CONVERSATION

SUPPOSED TO BE HELD BETWEEN MR. R., MRS. R.,
MISS R., AND MASTER R., ON NEW YEAR'S
MORNING, 1836.

Mr. R. What a time,—nearly nine!

Miss R. Breakfast's been a long time ready.

Mrs. R. What a wind from behind!

Mary can't have shut the door.

It is open, I am sure.

Go and shut it

Quickly.

Miss R.   But it,

Ma'am, is shut already.

Mrs. R. Is it close?   I suppose,

Then, it's something in the kitchen,—

Windows open,—doors ajar.

Lucy, Lucy! go and do see!

Lucy. Ma'am, there an't.

Mrs. R.   I'm sure there are.

Mr. R. You don't expect that at this time it

Can be any better!

Climate, climate,—only climate!

This is English weather!

Sharply here the winters close in ;

Here you know we can't complain
Of cold severe.

Master R.　　　　　　　Ponds all frozen!

Miss R. Hail and snow!

Master R.　　　　　　　Wind and rain!

Mr. R. Glass and bones all brittle!　I
Vex myself with thinking how
Fine the weather may be now
Far away in Italy.

Master R. Sky so blue over you!

Miss R. Moon so bright in the night!

Mr. R. There come neither clouds nor storm;

Master R. But lovely weather,

Miss R.　　{　　　　　　　Mild and warm.

Mrs. R. Ay; and poison in the air!
Better here than anywhere,—
Sitting at the breakfast-table,
Reading in your easy-chair.
All your party
Strong and hearty,
Gathered round a cheerful fire
Warmly blazing:—
'Tis amazing
That you grumble constantly!
Pray, what more would you desire?

Mr. R. Softer air and sunnier sky,
And a clime where no one knows
What it is to blow one's nose.
Ever since the Alps we crossed

—'Twas indeed a piece of folly—
We've been really tempest-tossed,—
Drenched with rain and pinched with frost.
Then the town's so melancholy !
People come for hours to chatter
Over every little matter ;—
My prices and my wine run down,—
This too pale, and that's too brown.—

Mrs. R. Yet they come in every day for it,
And you know you make them pay for it !

Mr. R. (*without noticing the interruption.*)
There behind my desk sit I,
Writing letters dull and dry ;
Or in the docks, I stand and shiver,
In the damp air of the river ;
Or in the docks where mingled are
Sawdust, cobwebs, oil and tar ;
Or on the quay, when London fog sheds
A yellow light on butts and hogsheads,
'Mid vessels, anchors, ropes, and bowsprits,—
I often find myself in low spirits.
And in the midst of it all, I
Think how very different
Were my employments when we went
Travelling in Italy ;—
Seeing churches, large and fair,—

Master R. Gems and marbles, rich and rare,—

Miss R. Palaces, of pictures quite full,—

Mr. R. Lakes and mountains,—

Master R.   Oh, delightful !

Mr. R. Distant Alps, and handsome cities ;
       Is it not a thousand pities
       That we are not there ?

Mrs. R. No, indeed !   I wonder to hear you !
       Don't you know, my dear, that here you
       Have the same thing every day,
       After getting through the first of it ?

Mr. R. Is not that just what I say ?
       That's the very worst of it !
       Not change, indeed !   I wish it would !

Mrs. R. I never knew a man so rude :
       You interrupt so !   Here, I say,
       You stoutly keep the cold at bay ;
       But there, on whistling wings the wind blows
       Through cracking walls and open windows,
       Bringing o'er the Adriatic,
       To the tourist so ecstatic,
       Colds, catarrhs, and pains rheumatic ;
       Or Sirocco from Morocco,
       With its poison-heated breath,
       Blows across the panting plain
       Cholera, and plague, and death.
       'Twould be an improvement, truly,
       On the cold that ends our year,
       If you'd take the cold more coolly,—
       Spring will soon be here !

Mr. R. [after a pause of reflection.]
       Travelling, I must allow,

Sometimes is a little cloying;
And has inconveniences,
Though perhaps they are not great,—
Rising early, riding late,—
Also, notes of one's expenses,
Which I always find annoying.
And though a wish for sunnier skies
Sometimes in one's mind will rise,
Vexing one a little, I
Think that one may spend as gay
A Christmas or a New-Year's-Day
In England, as in Italy!

[*End of December.*]

BIOGRAPHICAL DATA; 1826–1835.

1826; John Ruskin, 7 years of age on *Feb.* 8 : living at Herne Hill, wrote ' Needless Alarm" (*Jan.*) : visit to the English Lakes and Perth (*Summer*) suggested "Glen of Glenfarg" and "Farewell to Scotland" (*Sept.*). Returning to Herne Hill, studied Latin Grammar under his mother ; began "Harry and Lucy" (*Sept.* or *Oct.*) ; wrote "Time" (*Dec.*).

1827 ; age 8. At Herne Hill, continued " Harry and Lucy." In the summer, visited Perth ; fever at Dunkeld ; frosty morning in Glenfarg suggested " Papa, how pretty those icicles are" (*Autumn*). At Herne Hill, wrote "The Sun" (*Dec.*). His cousin Jessie died this winter.

1828 ; age 9. At Herne Hill, versified Scott's " Monastery ;" began "Eudosia ;" wrote "May," "Skiddaw," "Derwentwater" (*May*). Visited Plymouth and West of England (*Summer*). Death of his aunts at Croydon and Perth : his cousin Mary Richardson adopted by his parents. At Herne Hill, continued "Eudosia," and wrote New Year's poem, "Highland Music" (*Dec.* 31).

1829 ; age 10. At Herne Hill. wrote "The Yellow Fog." Illness in spring. First sketching from nature at Sevenoaks, Tunbridge (*middle of July*), Canterbury, Dover, and Battle Abbey.   During the tour, wrote "The Moon" (*June*), "Happiness" (*July*), and probably "Sabbath Morning" (*Aug.*).   At Herne Hill, "Shagram" and "Etna" (*Oct.*), and New Year's poem (*Dec.* 30).

1830 ; age 11.   At Herne Hill, wrote "Trafalgar" (*Feb.* 12) and "Dash" (*Ap.* 30).   Left London with his parents and cousin Mary (*Tuesday, May* 18) for the tour, partly described in "The Iteriad."   Saw the colleges at Oxford, pictures at Blenheim, Worcester Cathedral, Shakspere's home, Warwick Castle, Birmingham, Lichfield Cathedral, Matlock, Dovedale, and Haddon Hall (*Friday, June* 11).   Travelled by Manchester, Liverpool, Preston, Lancaster and Kendal to Low-wood, Windermere (*Tuesday, June* 22) ; on the Wednesday to Keswick ; on Sunday saw Southey at Crosthwaite Church ; on Monday, excursion to Buttermere ; on Wednesday (*June* 30), ascended Skiddaw ; on Thursday, went to Patterdale ; on Friday, returned to Low-wood ; on Sunday (*July* 4), saw Wordsworth at Rydal Chapel ; on Tuesday, took excursion to Coniston.   They left the Lakes on Monday, *July* 12, for Kendal and Kirkby Lonsdale ; revisited Haddon (*July* 16), and returned by Gloucester and Cheltenham to Herne Hill (*Sept.*).   During this tour he wrote a diary, collaborating with Mary Richardson ; and several poems not connected with the journey ; also, probably, "Haddon Hall."   On returning to Herne Hill, began Greek under Dr. Andrews ; copied Cruikshank's illustrations to Grimm ; wrote "On the Death of my Cousin Jessie" (*Sept.* 9) and "Ascent of Skiddaw" (*Nov.-Dec.*).

1831 ; age 12. At Herne Hill, continued "Iteriad ;" took first drawing-lessons from Mr. Runciman ; and began to read Byron. Wrote "The Fairies" and "To my Heart" (*Jan.*) ; "Poesie" and "Want of a Subject" (*March*). On *May* 25 started with the family on the Welsh tour, travelling by way of Dover, Margate, Southampton, Portsmouth, Stonehenge, Hereford, Devil's Bridge, Hafod, Aberystwith, Dolgelly, Cader Idris, Barmouth, Harlech, Carnarvon, Snowdon, Conway, Llangollen, Chepstow, Clifton, Newbury (*July* 21). During the tour, wrote "To the Ocean Spirits" and "To the Fairies" (*June* 20) ; and, suggested by Wales, on his return to Herne Hill, "The Eternal Hills" (*Oct.*), "Moonlight on the Mountains" (*Nov.* 30), and "Harlech Castle" (*Dec.*?). Began Mathematics (and probably French) under Mr. Rowbotham ; wrote "Bedtime" (*Sept.*) in the metre of "Don Juan ;" "To the Memory of Scott" (on Scott's leaving, invalided, for Italy) ; "The Site of Babylon," in imitation of Byron's "Hebrew Melodies ;" (*Nov.* 6,) and "Sonnet to a Cloud" (*end of year*).

1832 ; age 13. At Herne Hill, wrote "Sonnet : Morning," and "Southern Breeze" (*Feb.*) ; "Destruction of Pharaoh (*March*). Travelled to Sevenoaks and Dover (*May* 22–*June* 30) ; was at Hastings on *July* 19. On returning home wrote "The Grave of the Poet" (on hearing of Scott's death). This year he drew trees at Dulwich, and the bridge at Herne Hill ; and began a friendship with Richard Fall.

1833 ; age 14. At Herne Hill, wrote "I weary for the torrent leaping" (*Winter*). On his birthday (*Feb.* 8) received Rogers' "Italy," and began to study Turner.

About this time was introduced to James Hogg and Samuel Rogers, by Thomas Pringle. For summer tour, travelled with Mr. and Mrs. Ruskin, Mary Richardson, Ann his nurse, and Salvador their courier, to Calais (*May* 11), Cassel, Lille, Tournay, Brussels, Heidelberg, Constance, Splügen, Milan, Genoa, Turin, Great St. Bernard, Vevey, Interlachen, Chamouni, and Paris, where he copied Rembrandt's "Last Supper" in the Louvre, and met the Domecq family for the first time. Returned to Herne Hill (*Sep.* 21), and began a poetical account of the tour, with illustrations. Went to school to the Rev. Thomas Dale.

1834 ; age 15. His cousin Charles Richardson, who had introduced him to Pringle, drowned (*Jan.* 22). At Herne Hill, for birthday gift, he received Saussure's "Voyages dans les Alpes" (*Feb.* 8). Published in Loudon's *Mag. of Natural History* a "Letter on the Colour of the Rhine" and "Mont Blanc and Twisted Strata" (*March*). Continued the "Tour," and wrote "The Crystal-Hunter" (*May*). This spring, he was studying poetry after Byron, drawing after Turner, architecture after Prout, geology after Saussure, and mineralogy after Jameson and at the British Museum ; beside school-work,—classics under Dale, and mathematics under Rowbotham. During the summer holidays he visited Windsor, Oxford, Cheltenham, Malvern, and Salisbury (*June* 30–*July* 23) ; then returned to school ; and wrote "Invention of Quadrilles" and "The Months" (*Dec.*).

1835 ; age 16. At Herne Hill ; taken from school by pleurisy in *Spring.* Left home for summer tour (*June* 2) by

Dover, Calais, Paris, Geneva, Chamouni, St. Bernard, Aosta, Swiss Oberland, Bormio, Verona, Venice (*Oct.* 6–12), Salzburg, Carlsruhe, Strasburg, Paris, London (*Dec.* 10). During the tour, sketched and wrote "Poetical Journal," "Letter to R. Fall," &c. Published in "Friendship's Offering" for 1835 "Salzburg," "Andernach," "St. Goar ;" wrote "The Avalanche," "Emigration of the Sprites," &c., and "Conversation" (*Dec.*) at Herne Hill. With this year closes the first period of his poetical activity, that of his boyhood, in which he remained under the influences of a limited domestic circle, and wrote verse on the models afforded him by Scott and Byron.

PRELIMINARY NOTE ON THE ORIGINAL MSS. OF THE POEMS.

THE early writings of Mr. Ruskin were carefully preserved by his parents, who encouraged, though they do not seem to have supervised, the production of his juvenile attempts. In only two or three instances a word has been crossed out, and an emendation substituted by his father ; but in several places his father and mother have inserted dates into the note-books, or endorsed a loose sheet "John's Poetry, (*Date.*)" There is no trace of subsequent revision on the author's part of any poems, except those which actually appeared in print during his youth.

Some of the MSS. are very beautifully written in "copper-plate" or "print" hand : indeed, the fair-copying seems to have been quite as important a business as the invention and versification, which were apparently spontaneous, and— to judge from the comparatively small amount of interlinea-tion—almost improvisational. But in the rough original drafts the writing is difficult to read ; and, as a single poem was often composed in fragments, at different times, inter-spersed between all sorts of other writings, the MSS. present a very chaotic appearance.

After some study of these ancient Codices, and of their Palæography—for they present a complete sequence of the phases of Mr. Ruskin's handwriting from the earliest period —the Editor has been able to disentangle their contents and to arrange them in chronological order ; which it may be worth while to note here, both for the assistance of future students, and in justification of the hypothetical dates assigned to some of the poems.

No. I. Ruled note-book, bound in red leather ; 6 by nearly 4 inches ; pp. 88, of which 77 (numbered wrongly up to 96) contain " Harry and Lucy" (See *Præterita*, I. iii. p. 77), and the rest, the six poems mentioned in the introduction to the present work. The book was begun in *September* or *October* 1826, and finished in *January* 1827. One at least of the poems had been written before the book was begun.

No. II. Home-made book of plain paper, no cover ; nearly 6½ by 4 inches ; pp. 32 ; consisting in rough drafts of poems, " Harry and Lucy," and letters to his father and Mrs. Monro, also notes on sermons. This belongs to the first half of 1828.

No. III. Red book, uniform with No. I., but containing only 84 pp. This is confusedly put together at different periods. (*a.*) The title-page bears " Harry and Lucy (&c.) vol. II.," begun in 1827 as sequel to No. I. (*b.*) Simultaneously with the prose story, on p. 62 begins a collection of previously written verses under the heading "poetry discriptive" (*sic*), lasting to p. 70. (*c.*) Then the author turned back, and, about New Year 1828, to judge from the writing as well as from the entries, continued the same collection from p. 21 to p. 33. (*d.*) Then he filled the end of the volume with two "Books" of "The Monastery" (Scott's novel versified). (*e.*) Having reached the last page, he turned back to p. 52 for " Book 3 ; " and " Book 4" ends incomplete on p. 58. This poem was written during the first half of 1828. (*f.*) Finally, in *March* 1829 this volume was taken up again, and pp. 36–50 were filled with miscellaneous verses. No. III., therefore, dates from 1827 to 1829.

No. IV. Red book, similar to Nos. I. and III., containing

title and pp. 17 of "Eudosia" (Præt. I. iii. p. 89–91); followed by Mr. J. J. Ruskin's catalogue, compiled in after years, of his son's published poems; beginning with the entry, "On Skiddaw and Derwentwater; page 72, *Spiritual Times, Feby.* 1831, age 11 years;" and ending in the year 1846 with the note that he had been "compared with Goethe, Coleridge, J. Taylor, Burke, Juvenal." The end of the book contains mineralogy-notes, as mentioned in Præt. (*loc. cit.*).

No. V. Ruled note-book; greenish marbled boards, half-bound in chocolate calf, gilt; $7\frac{1}{4}$ by $4\frac{3}{4}$ inches; pp. 167 numbered, of which 138 are filled in a very neat "print" hand: no title; p. 1 headed "MISCELLANEOUS POETRY," to which his father has subjoined "*By J. Ruskin from 10 years to 11 to 12 to   of age.*" The poems are nearly all dated, and range from *June* 28, 1829, to *February* 1832. The dates are probably those of production, for they are slightly inconsecutive; which would not be the case if they were dates of entry; and, when chronologically arranged, they tally with the order of the first drafts in No. VI.

No. VI. Tall ruled note-book; $12\frac{1}{2}$ by $4\frac{1}{2}$ inches; reddish marbled paper covers, of which one and 57 pp. have been torn away, leaving pp. 80. This was a rough-copy book, begun at the commencement of 1830. It contains first drafts of poems copied into No. V., and of the "Iteriad" and others; and serves until *September* or *October* 1831. Later on, in 1838, it was taken up and used for a rough copy of the "Essay on the Comparative Advantages of Music and Painting" (on which see Præt. I. xii. p. 409). And at the end, the book being turned round, begins anew with a prose story, "Macbeth." It has an incomplete Index, showing that pp. 1–57 contained poems, now lost, on "Bonaparte," "Greek," "Ghost of Old English Roast-beef," "Ivanhoe," "London Streets," "Lion," "To Myself," "Revolution," "Senna Tea,"

"Salamis ;" as well as a number of poems preserved in No. V., dating from *February* 1, 1830, to January 5, 1831.

No. VII. (in the possession of Mrs. Arthur Severn). Ruled note-book, greenish marbled paper boards, half-bound in dark blue leather ; 10 by 8½ inches : pp. 1–115 occupied by the "Iteriad," and six more by an unfinished poem on "Athens." The whole is written in a fair "copperplate" hand, with flourished Gothic titles. The book, being reversed, contains pp. 23 of Mr. Ruskin's writings copied in a female hand, perhaps Mary Richardson's, beginning with "The Rhine" and "Chamouni" from the tour of 1833 ; also part of "Mont Blanc" and the "Rhyming Letter to Richard Fall ' (end of *Oct.* 1836). It contains also an essay which I make no doubt is the long-lost *Reply to the Criticism on Turner in Blackwood's Magazine,* "of which," its author said in 1886, "I wish I could now find any fragment" (Præt. I. xii. p. 400). It bears date *Oct.* 1. 1836, and is highly interesting as the germ, both in subject and style, of "Modern Painters." I am happy in the permission to print this and other early unpublished prose writings in a companion volume to these Poems.

No. VIII. Ruled note-book ; reddish paper boards, half-bound in black leather ; 9¼ by 5¾ inches ; pp. 272 and fly-leaves. This contains rough copies of poems, beginning at the end of *September* or early in *October* 1831, and ending in 1838, including the prose story of "Leoni" in first draft. The volume is very confused in its stratification ; but I believe the following to be the true sequence of the formations unconformably exposed in it :—(*a.*) Pp. 1–53 contain verses ranging from the later part of "Iteriad, Book 4," up to "The Month of May" (*May* 10, 1833). (*b.*) After the summer tour to Switzerland and Italy it was taken up again, and the prose and verse description of that tour was begun on p. 54. (*c.*)

But before half the projected quantity had been composed, the author had occasion to write the New Year's address to his father for 1835; and so, leaving as many pages as he calculated would be full space for the remainder of the "Tour," he began afresh on p. 168 with the poem from which "The Months" is extracted; following with other occasional verse, including "The Avalanche" and "The Emigration of the Sprites," and ending with the Birthday Address to his Father, *May* 10, 1836. (*d.*) Meanwhile, the 1833 "Tour" was abandoned, and was followed on p. 106 by some poems descriptive of a new Tour—that of 1835; and, on entering 1836, by the poems to "Adèle" and "Leoni." This section ends, on p. 167, with "Memory;—The Summer Wind is soft and kind," dated in "Poems. J. R." *Ætat.* 19 (*i.e.*, 1838). It is a surprise to go on from that, on the next page, to section (*c.*) in earlier handwriting, and a poem indubitably written in 1834! (*e.*) Farther, on p. 194, the unfinished play of "Marcolini" was begun, in the summer of 1836, and occupies the next section of the volume. (*f.*) Lastly, the book, being reversed, contains occasional poems which I attribute to *May–December*, 1834; *i.e.*, written *after* the Birthday-poem of 1834, which occurs in the middle of the 1833 "Tour," and *before* he began his plan of the fresh section (*c.*). This section (*f.*) includes "The Invention of Quadrilles."

No. IX. (in the possession of Mrs. Arthur Severn). Thick, ruled note-book; brown marbled boards, half-bound in bluish-green leather; 8 by 6½ inches. Pp. 1-21 are prepared for alphabetical index: pp. 22-23 contain quotations in Mrs. J. J. Ruskin's handwriting,—"Advice of his mother to the Chevalier Bayard," and I. Chronicles xxviii. 9. Pp. 25-111, about a third of the book, were filled with prose and verse in a good "copperplate" hand, and with inserted drawings illustrating his tour of the year before. It is about this book that he says (Præt. I. iv. p. 130),—"The winter of '33, and what time I could steal to amuse myself in, out of '34, were spent in composing, writing fair, and drawing vignettes for the decoration of the aforesaid poetical account of our tour, in imitation of Rogers' Italy. The drawings were made on separate pieces of paper and pasted into the books [*book*]; many have since been taken out, others are there for which the verses were never written, for I had spent my fervour before I got up the Rhine. I leave the unfinished folly in Joanie's care, that none but friends may see it." The "folly" I understand to refer, not to the literary quality of the verse, but to the miscalculation and miscarriage of an ambitious project; for, as I find from a list at the end of No. VIII., he had intended this volume to contain about 150 pieces of prose and poetry, and at least as many drawings! And in saying he did not follow his tour beyond the Rhine, Mr. Ruskin refers only to this volume, No. IX. I am pretty certain that he was not aware of the amount of material existing in rough copies at the back of his book-shelves.

No. X. (in the possession of Mrs. Arthur Severn). A cover containing :—

(*a*.) "Journal [by John Ruskin and Mary Richardson] of a Tour to the Lakes in 1830;" in two paper books = 44 + 20 pages.

(*b*.) The Poetical Tour of 1835, in two paper books; Canto I. = pp. 26; Canto II. as far as carried = pp. 10.

(*c*.) Letter from Abroad to Richard Fall (1835); 5 large pages, double columns.

(*d*.) "Conversation supposed to be held on New Year's Day 1836"; pp. 6.

(*e*.) Letter to his Father in verse; the original, with post-mark—(MR. 31, 1836).

(*f.*) Part of " The Exile of St. Helena ;" a poem se
the Newdigate Prize, 1838 ; lines 1–185 = pp. 7.

And other papers, not in verse.

No. XI. An envelope containing collected loose
including poems ; fair-copied by the author as p
chiefly to his father ; or copied by others.   Th
useful as fixing dates in some cases ; *e.g.*, the New
Address, 1827 ; and as supplying corrections or addi
other instances.

Of the published poems, only a few exist in MS.
them have been transcribed by Miss Allen from Mr.
Allen's copy of "Poems. J. R."; privately printed
now excessively rare.   "Salzburg," "Andernach," a
Goar" have been taken from "Friendship's Offering
—the copy inscribed "To John Ruskin from the Pub
Full account of the published poems has been given
Thomas J. Wise in his "Bibliography of the Writings
John Ruskin," part 1, *Sept.* 1889 (printed for sub
only) ; of which I have gladly availed myself.

NOTES TO THE POEMS.

Note I. "Glenfarg" (p. 4).—In "The Queen of the Air" (iii. 12) Mr. Ruskin gives *January* 1, 1828, as the date (and Mr. Wise follows him ; "Bibliography," p. 29). But this is the date of the *next* poem in Note-book No. III. ; from the description of which, above, it appears that section (*c.*)—in which "Glenfarg" occurs—though written about *January* 1828, contains poems of earlier periods ; that preceding "Glenfarg" goes so far back as *January* 1, 1827, as proved by a copy in No. XI. Now "The Sun," though dated *January* 1, 1828, was prepared beforehand as a New Year's Address to his father ; and thus the *earlier* piece, "Glenfarg," is put at any rate into 1827. The occasion was some autumnal frost, occurring before the author had left Scotland after his summer visit ; though the poem was probably written on his return to Herne Hill for the winter. (See Biographical Data for 1827.)

Note II. "The Sun" (p. 5).—"Constantly in the garden when the weather was fine, my time there was passed chiefly in close watching of the ways of plants. I had not the smallest taste for growing them, or taking care of them. . . . The old gardener only came once a week, for what sweeping and weeding needed doing ; I was fain to learn to sweep the walks with him, but was discouraged and shamed by his always doing the bits that I had done over again. I was extremely fond of digging holes, but that form of gardening was not allowed." (*Præterita*, I. iii. p. 88.)

Note III. "May" (p. 9).--Under the instructions which have been given him, the Editor prints only such verses as are of sufficient completeness to stand alone. Birthday Addresses usually need lopping to be presentable as "poems ;" and the right place to print these fragments *in extenso*, if ever this be called for, would be in a detailed biography. One piece, sketched in the spring of 1828, before *May*, and fair-copied in No. III. section (*f.*), *March* 1829, contains some lines appreciating the British man-of-war as in "Harbours of England," and too prophetic of "The Crown of Wild Olive" to be altogether omitted :—

> "Those sails that sometimes pleasing zephyrs fill,
> And sometimes Boreas blows with all his force,
> Now at the present time look fair and sweet ;
> But who can tell the future in a day ?
> Perhaps those sails are tattered rags, shot through
> With many a ball,—half dropping from their yards.
> —Then those destructive rows of huge machines,—
> *Destructive in their making,—in their use !*
> O War, what causes thee the curse of man ?
> 'Tis avarice and ambition, kindred vices ;
> *'Tis vice, not war, that is the curse of man.*"

Note IV. "Skiddaw" (p. 11), "Derwentwater" (p. 13). These are deciphered from note-book No. II., where they occur in a childish and almost illegible scribble. I have not mended them, except by omission of incomplete parts, and by the insertion of the author's own after-thoughts : *e.g.* line 19 of "Skiddaw" in its final state occurs among the lines of "Derwentwater." These pieces were written at Herne Hill, I think in May, as part of the Birthday Address ; for after them comes the conclusion of the Birthday letter :

"a letter on your birthday, but this is merely wasting paper when there is no need for it. But, papa, alas I have just been up to mama, and she says not to make such a long letter. So, papa, good-bye, Mr. papa, your affectionate son John Ruskin."

The references to Eolus and Penelope seem to show that he was familiar not only with Pope's Iliad (Præt. I. iii. p. 76), but with the Odyssey also. The octosyllabics concluding " Derwentwater" show the early influence of Scott, as the heroic couplets of " Eudosia" betray that of Pope. Mr. Ruskin does not say anything of Southey as an influence of his early years ; no doubt he received no impulse of *thought* from the then Laureate, but he admired him (see " Iteriad," p. 63), and probably caught the anapæstic metres from him.

To the poems of this year must be added the New Year's gift to his father, dated December 31, 1828, facsimiled in the Illustrated Edition as specimen of handwriting ; perhaps a fragment of " The Monastery " (see the novel, chap. 35).

[HIGHLAND MUSIC.]

But frightened was the preacher when
He heard all echoed down the glen
The music of the clans.
'Twas martial music, and around
Well echoed was the beauteous sound
By valley, rock, and hill.
It died away upon his ear,
And spread abroad, now there, now here,
And gathered strength again. (Qy. for *amain* ?)
And now the flute, and now the drum,
Mingling upon the winds they come,
And die away again.
Another strain, another sound,
And now 'tis silence all around ;—
The martial music's gone !

Note in his father's handwriting :—" See Chronicles of the Canongate ; the Flute & Drum & Bagpipe ; the latter having no Beauty."

Note V. "Eudosia" (p. 15).—The date given by the author (Præt. I. iii. p. 89) is that of the beginning of the fair copy. As far as Book I. line 160 was drafted before the Birthday Address in Note-book No. II. "Eudosia" must therefore have been commenced in March or April 1828. The name no doubt refers to the "good gifts" of creation, as the motto on the title-page is "These are Thy glorious works, Parent of good, Almighty! Thine this universal frame, Thus wondrous fair.—Milton." The author's account of Book I. quoted on p. 15 and in notes pp. 16, 17, is fully sufficient ; for the rest of it is simply a versified catalogue of flowers and trees ; perorating, however, in a description of the oak and its uses, not without a touch of epic feeling :

> " Now the broad Oak displays its arms around ;
> Its brawny branches, spreading, sweep the ground :
> Its kingly arms their giant strength display,—
> With their great breadth e'en hide the face of day,
> Broad round the mother-trunk they throw their arms,
> And dare encounter dreadful war's alarms.
> To their assistance England owes her strength ;
> The spoils of nations come from their dread length.
> Of them are formèd England's wooden walls ;
> With them surrounded, England loves Mars' calls.   .
> In vain the waves attempt to break their sides,
> And to o'erwhelm them with the rushing tides. . . .
> Foaming with rage that mortals should surmount
> The wat'ry deep, and sail the seas about.
> Unheeding of their rage, the Oak sails on ;
> And Britons triumphing o'er seas are borne."

Note VI. "The Yellow Fog" (p. 23).—This may have been written at any time during the winter of 1828–29. It was copied in March 1829 in Note-book No. III. section (*f.*).   In line 15, "*new* light" may be read "*now* light."

Note VII. "The Moon" (p. 25).—Now begins Note-book

No. V., in which the materials are carefully written and frequently dated.

Note VIII. "Shagram" (p. 28).—A Shetland pony : the name is taken from Sir W. Scott's "Monastery," chap iii., and occurs in the paraphrase of the novel,—a childish production of the early part of 1828, already mentioned ; of which the following is a sufficient specimen :—

> "There was a bog, and o'er this part,
> Where even the light-footed hart
> Go could not, for his feet in clay
> Sank as he sped him on his way,
> Not only Martin had to pass,
> But e'en good Shagram with the lass. . . .
> He to Shagram began to say
> 'Come on, good horse, and let us see
> Whether thou'lt obey thy master,—me !
> Come on !' But Shagram would not go ;
> Though mute, he very well said 'No !'"

Note IX. "Trafalgar" (p. 35).—In the last line but one, "weep" may be a clerical error for "grieve."   There is no rough copy.   In the early part of 1830 the author's poetical activity was great ; but "Trafalgar" and "Dash" are much the most presentable pieces of this period.

Note X. "Dash" (p. 38).—Dash was the brown and white spaniel belonging to Mrs. Richardson of Croydon, the author's aunt.   At her death, he lay beside her body and on her coffin till they were taken away from him ; then he was brought to Herne Hill in 1828 (Præt. I. v. p. 140).   He was still in existence in 1836 ; see the "Letter" of March 31 in that year (vol. ii. of these Poems), and was several times commemorated in verse.   One bit of doggerel, though not finding a place among the poems of 1831, may be admitted

here, as illustrating Mr. Ruskin's fondness for dogs (a
compare the story of Wisie, Præt. II. ii. pp. 52–57) :

DASH.

1.

Was there ever like Dashy
A dog half so splashy,
Amid all the species canine ?
Or even so good ?
Though he sometimes with mud
Defiles his hair, white as the foam of the brine :
No other dog equals the dog that is mine !

2.

There never was one
Half so good at a bone,—
So nicely and neatly he gnaws it,—
As if he were starving !
He don't care a farthing
For the spit and the phiz [fizz] of the cat as she claws it
But from her our Dash most successfully paws it.

3.

Upon his hind-legs
Most politely he begs
For any nice stray bit of meat, sir !
You cannot resist him,
He has such a system,
As he looks in your face, and jumps up on your seat, si
That you give him a nice bit of something to eat, sir !

4.

With looks quite appealing,—
It quite hurts his feeling
If you but attempt for to fondle the cat, sir ;
Kicks up such a row ;
And he will not allow
That you should but give her a comforting pat, sir,
Or stroke, while she's purring, the fur of her back, sir !

5.

He has been a fine round ;
For twice lost and twice found
In the city of London the dogy has been,
And you may opine, sir,
How tedious the time, sir,
Appeared, that rolled on those same periods between !
What a pity he can't tell us what he has seen !

6.

But I've said enough,
Lest you think this a puff,
Though he really deserveth to be, sir, a bust in ; *
And if you want my name,
Why, dear sir, I remain
A praiser of Dash, who delighteth a crust in,
And your most obedient, wee Johnny Ruskin.

16 *November*, 1831.

Note XI. "Haddon Hall" (p. 39).—The itinerary and dates of this tour of 1830 are given in the Biographical Notes above. The author in his prose journal mentions the old armour at Haddon, and "the dishes which were served up to table, of which the largest was about two feet long, and the smallest about a foot. These were soup-plates, which at a moderate computation were about eight inches deep. We then," he continues, "saw the great dining-hall. There were originally three large tables, but only one remains."

Note XII. "On the Death of my Cousin Jessie" (p. 40.) She died nearly three years earlier. The poem is Ossianic in form, as being intended for the 'coronach' of a *Highland* girl (Præt. I. iii. 95).

Note XIII. "Ascent of Skiddaw" (p. 42).—Wednesday,

* *i.e.* "to be put in a bust," sculptured.

June 30, 1830.   In his journal the author notes, "We were very fortunate in the day, as we might have gone up a hundred times, and not have had the view we had that day." The *brandy* (pp. 42, 45), chronicled with juvenile roguishness, was in those times indispensable to so adventurous an ascent. Jonathan Otley in his guide-book (1834) describing Skiddaw, mentions "the brandy, which—with a few biscuits or sandwiches—a provident guide will not fail to recommend." The poem was written at Herne Hill in November and December, and copied into Note-book No. V. above the date of *Dec.* 26, 1830.   Afterwards the rest of the tour was versified and the whole copied into No. VII., under the title of "The Iteriad ; or, Three Weeks among the Lakes." This, if printed without omissions, would occupy a space quite disproportionate to its value.   I have selected the passages "From Kendal to Low-wood" as far as "Keswick" from Book I., written *January* to *March ;* "Friar's Crag" as far as "Buttermere" from Book II., written *March* to *May ;* and the rest from Book IV., written *July* to *September.*

Note XIV. "Kendal to Low-wood" (p. 51).—Tuesday, *June* 22, 1830.   "Low-wood Inn was then little more than a country cottage, and Ambleside a rural village ; and the absolute peace and bliss which any one who cared for grassy hills and for sweet waters might find at every footstep, and at every turn of crag or bend of bay, was totally unlike anything I ever saw, or read of elsewhere " (Præt. I. v. p. 155).

Note XV. "Grasmere" (p. 54).—The journey from Low-wood by Grasmere and Thirlmere to Keswick was taken on Wednesday, *June* 23, 1830.   They put up at the "Royal Oak," at Keswick.

Note XVI. "Friar's Crag and Castle-head" (p. 58) were visited on Thursday, *June* 24, 1830. The author had already received strong impressions of the same scenery. "The first thing which I remember as an event in life (meaning, I suppose, my first memory of things afterwards chiefly precious to me, Præt. I. v. p. 154) was being taken by my nurse to the brow of Friar's Crag on Derwentwater; the intense joy, mingled with awe, that I had in looking through the hollows in the mossy roots, over the crag, into the dark lake, has associated itself more or less with all twining roots of trees ever since" (Modern Painters, vol. iii. part iv. chap. 17, § 13). The next day they visited Crosthwaite's museum, and the Saturday was wet.

Note XVII. "Hero-worship" (p. 63).—Mary Richardson writes in the Journal: "On Sunday we went to Crosthwaite Church, which is about a mile from the town of Keswick. We were put into a seat that would have been a disgrace to any church, it was so dirty." At this point her cousin John takes up the story, and continues: "But we easily put up with that, as in the seat directly opposite Mr. Southey sat. We saw him very nicely. He seemed extremely attentive; and by what we saw of him, we should think him very pious. He has a very keen eye, and looks extremely like—a poet." On the next Sunday, they saw Wordsworth at Rydal Chapel, and "were rather disappointed in this gentleman's appearance."

Note XVIII. "Borrowdale" (p. 64), and "Buttermere" (p. 68).—This excursion was taken on Monday, *June* 28. There is no mention in the Journal of the thunderstorm, but only of the wet.

Note XIX. "Ullswater" (P. 70).—The journey to Patter-
dale from Keswick was made on Thursday, *July* 1.

Note XX. "Kirkstone" (p. 73).—They returned to Low-
wood on Friday, *July* 2, and stayed there until *July* 10:
leaving the Lakes on the 12th. "The house which we
saw,"—Brathay Hall. Forty years later, Mr. Ruskin got
"such a house," and got it without stultifying his early
ideal ; for though he has added to Brantwood, the original
house is an old one.

Note XXI. "Coniston" (p. 74).—This was not the author's
first introduction to Coniston ; he had visited it in 1824 and
1826, if not oftener : indeed, the minuteness and accuracy
of the descriptions in the "Iteriad" evince more familiarity
with the Lake District than could have been gained in this
hasty tour,—at least they are much ampler than the descrip-
tions in the Journal. "The inn at Coniston was then actually
at the upper end of the lake, the road from Ambleside to the
village passing just between it and the water ; and the view
of the long reach of lake, with its loftly wooded lateral hills,
had for my father a tender charm which excited the same
feeling as that with which he afterwards regarded the lakes
of Italy" (Præt. I. v. p. 155). On this visit, *July* 6, 1830, the
Journal notes : "We had some very fine char for dinner. . .
Although it was a wet day, we enjoyed ourselves very much."
The char satisfactorily accounts for the heavy bill.

Note XXII. "To Poesie" (p. 82).—Next in chronological
order before this poem comes a piece facsimiled in the Illus-
trated Edition as follows :—

THE FAIRIES.

1.

I wandered forth at midnight,
And silently, silently rove
Where the moonlight poured
On the dewy sward,
And on the elfin grove.
'Twas a kind of fairy scenery,—
A kind of airy dreamery,—
Such silence as I love.

2.

When from the wood around me
The elfin circles skim,
Hand in hand
They join the band,
And in the dances swim.
And there they bounded merrily,
While sailing round me giddily,
And breezy numbers sing.

3.

How softly, softly murmuring
In sinking cadence low !
And now they seem
Of joy to sing,
And now to sing of woe :
As sweetly, sweetly whispering,
Those carols greet me listening,
And harmoniously flow.

4.

Thus rang the song :—" Ye fairies,
Now swiftly, swiftly bound,
Ere yet the day
In twilight grey

Shall send its light around !
Spring o'er the dewdrop shivering ;
Touch not the grass-blade quivering,
While vaulting from the ground !

5.

"Still circling on the green-sward,
Exert your nimble feet !
Dance, dance away,
Ye fairies gay,
And ply your footsteps fleet !
Ye sprites, ye elfins, wantoning,
Amongst the cowslips frolicking,
Here let your dances meet."

January 5, 1831.

Note XXIII. "To the Ocean-Spirits" (p. 87).—This and
the following were written in Wales (see Biographical Notes
for 1831) "The Eternal Hills," written at Herne Hill about
October, was probably inspired by Snowdon. "My first
sight of bolder * scenery was in Wales . . We went . . .
to Llanberis and up Snowdon" (Præt. I. v. p. 157). "Harlech
Castle" was another reminiscence of this tour ; and "Moon-
light on the Mountains" is quite Snowdonian in character.

Note XXIV. "Bed-Time" (p. 92).—"A master was found
for me to teach me mathematics. Mr. Rowbotham was an
extremely industrious, deserving, and fairly well-informed
person in his own branches, who . . . kept a 'young
gentlemen's Academy' near the Elephant and Castle.
Under the tuition, twice a week in the evening, of Mr.
Rowbotham, I prospered fairly in 1834" (Præt. I. iv. p. 133).
I venture to suggest that it must have been before 1834 that

Bolder, that is, than Skiddaw or Coniston Old Man as seen from
below.   He had not seen the grander mountain-crags of the Lake Dis-
trict at close quarters from the Eskdale or Wastdale side.

Mr. Rowbotham began to teach the author, since this poem, from its style, handwriting, and position in Note-book No. VI., must certainly be dated about *September* 1831. The mis-spelling of the name (Roebotham) looks as though he were quite a new acquaintance. The metre shows the first definite trace of Byron's influence ; he had begun to read Byron early in this year.

Note XXV. "To the Memory of Sir W. Scott" (p. 94).—Sir Walter had left Scotland in the previous month, *September* 1831 ; and was not expected to survive long. His death is commemorated in "The Grave of the Poet" (p. 110).

Note XXVI. "The Destruction of Pharaoh" (p. 109). This and "The Site of Babylon" seem to be modelled on the "Hebrew Melodies," and exhibit a more sonorous and *intellectual* style, derived from Byron (Præt. I. viii. pp. 257–266), which displaces the earlier juvenile jingle. After writing "The Site of Babylon" on *Nov.* 6, he began "The Destruction of Nineveh ;" but gave that up for "The Destruction of Pharaoh ;" the first attempt at which was a failure, and was dropped for a translation from Anacreon, whom he was reading with Dr. Andrews at the time (Præt. I. iv. p. 117). Then, after "The Southern Breeze," occurs "Mourn, Mizraim, Mourn," not dated, but earlier than the Birthday Address of the year (*May*). It is worth while precising the date of so fine a fragment.

Note XXVII. "I weary for the torrent leaping" (P. 115).—The earliest published poem ; not the *first* published. It begins "Poems. J. R." (pp. 3–4), and is quoted at length in "John Ruskin," &c., by W. E. A. Axon, 1879, pp. 6–5 (2nd edit., 1881, pp. 6–7) ; also in *Papers of the Manchester Literary*

Club, vol. v., 1879, pp. 156–157.   It is dated in "Poems. J. R." *Aetat.* 14 ; but from the position of the rough draft in Note-book No. VIII., it seems to have been written some time before the author actually reached the age of fourteen, *i.e.*, in his fourteenth year.   In Stanza 4, *Loweswater's dell* reads in the original draft *Glaramara's dell;* a reading which I wish I could restore, for the sake both of the sound and of the sense. The *dells* or coves of Glaramara are its striking features. Wordsworth's line should surely read "Murmuring from Glaramara's inmost *coves*," not *caves*, of which there are none. This song was suggested by the fact that the author had not been among mountains that year, but only to Dover and Hastings.   It is curious that his mountain-yearning does not carry him back to Snowdon, but to earlier visions of the Lake Country, his first and last mountain-love.

Note XXVIII. "Tour on the Continent, 1833" (p. 119).— The various sources, and the projected illustrated edition of these poems, are described in the Preliminary Notes under Nos. VII., VIII., IX., and XI.   The poems were not all written in 1833, nor in the order of places visited ; nor is the account of the tour in *Præterita* quite accurate ; for the travellers went to the west of Switzerland and the Oberland after being in Italy.   The second line of "Calais" reads in the original, "The ocean barrier is beating," which must be a mis-transcription of an insufficiently altered rough copy, now lost, as the reading is neither rhyme nor reason. The very few emendations I have presumed to make are marked by square brackets.

Note XXIX. " Cassel" (p. 120).—Omer = St. Omer, where is the Seminary, which suggests the religious procession. In the next piece "Lille," on p. 123, the "*Saxon* arch" betrays the student, till then, of architecture exclusively English. In "Brussels," on p. 125, "July's dreadful night" refers to Quatre Bras and Waterloo; a reminiscence of "Childe Harold."

Note XXX. "Andernach" (p. 128), first printed in "Friendship's Offering," 1835, pp. 317-318; omitted in "Poems. J. R.;" printed in the American edition of Ruskin's Poems, pp. 4-5. It is so much altered from the original draft that it may be interesting to compare the two versions.

First Sketch of "Andernach."

We have wound a weary way;
Twilight's mists are gathering grey.
Purple now the hills are showing;
Bright the western clouds are glowing.
Lashing on with giant force,
Rolls the Rhine his sullen course;
Flash his waves with flamy red,
Eddying o'er their basalt bed;—
Now with wide expanded breast,
Now between the hills compressed:
Ever noble, ever free,
Flows his river-majesty.
Now upon the evening skies
Andernach's grey ruins rise,—
Memorials of the Roman power;—
Buttress and battlement and tower,
Decaying, falling fast away,
The monuments of Cæsar's sway,—
In heaps together loosely thrown,—
The sculptured head, inscriptioned stone:
Unguarded now the bridge's length,
And failing fast its arches' strength;
The green sod in the moat is growing,
The cold wind in the chambers blowing,
And, flapping through the thin night-air,
The owl and bat, the tenants there.

Note XXXI. "Ehrenbreitstein" (p. 129).—Printe
"Poems. J. R." (pp. 8-12), and dated *Ætat.* 16 ; but cer
written earlier, as it occurs in Note-book VII., dated 1

Note XXXII. "St. Goar" (p. 133).—Published in "Fi
ship's Offering," 1835, pp. 318-319. Omitted in "P
J. R." Published in the American edition, pp. 5-6.
this, as in the case of Andernach, it may be interesti
compare the first draft ; if for nothing else, to show
the young poet could polish when he chose, and th
would have eliminated the slipshod grammar and
rhymes if he had prepared the rest of his juvenile vers
publication.

FIRST SKETCH OF "ST. GOAR."

We past a rock, whose bare front ever
Had borne the brunt of wind and weather ;
And downwards by the Rhine we bore
Upon the village of St. Goar,
That, 'mid the hills embosomed, lay
Where the Rhine checked his onward way,
And lay the mighty crags between ;
As if, enamoured of the scene,
He loved not on his way to wind,
And leave a scene so fair behind.
For grim the chasm through whose cleft
The waters had a passage reft ;
And gaunt the gorge that yawned before,
Through which, emerging, they must roar.
No marvel they should love to rest,
And peaceful spread their placid breast,
Before in fury driving dread,
Tormented on their rocky bed ;
Or flinging far their scattering spray
O'er the peaked rocks, that barred their way,
Wave upon wave at random tossed,
Or in the giddy whirlpool lost,

And now are undisturbed sleeping,—
No more on rocks those billows beating ;
But, lightly laughing, laps the tide,
Where stoop the vineyards to his side.

Note XXXIII. "Heidelberg" (p. 134).—The passage on
p. 136, "But climbed the cloud—the pine-trees tall," is in
the rough draft, but not in the fair copy. I restore it for the
sake of the fine "Turner" sky and effect. This poem is
apparently unfinished.

Note XXXIV. "The Black Forest" (p. 138).—"Kehl,"
line 2, is my conjecture ; the word in the original is illegible.
The poem must refer to the day's journey described in Præt.
I. vi. pp. 190–193 :—"Earliest morning saw us trotting over
the bridge of boats to Kehl, and in the eastern light I well
remember watching the Black Forest hills enlarge and rise
as we crossed the plain of the Rhine."

Note XXXV. "Entrance to Schaffhausen" (p. 140).—See
Præt. I. vi. p. 193. "It was past midnight when we reached
her closed gates," &c. The whole tour is well re-told in
Præterita; and the two accounts are worth comparing,
written as they are at an interval of more than fifty years
apart,—the one in verse and the other in prose,—and the
latter with a power of recollective imagination resembling
that of Turner.

Note XXXVI. "Evening at Chamouni" (p. 161).—It is
hardly necessary to remind the reader that this refers to the
first ascent of Mont Blanc in 1786 by Jacques Balmat.

Note XXXVII. "The Crystal-Hunter" (p. 167).—Written
for his father's birthday ; a sort of fantasia upon the scenery

and mineralogy in which the author had revelled the year before. The "Argument" seems to be that a crystal-hunter from a valley in the neighbourhood of Mont Blanc—born in Val Anzasca, but not necessarily starting thence—finds a cavern through which he penetrates into the valley of Chamouni, unknown before, but thereupon colonised. With this argument it is inconsistent that he claims to have anticipated Mr. Dent on the Dru ; but the letter introducing the poem (in the original MS.) offers it as "fables, froth ;" and it is worthy of a place, though unpolished in style, as an enthusiastic myth with a sober moral.

Note XXXVIII. "The Months" (p. 176).—Part of a New Year's address to his father. Published in "Friendship's Offering," 1836, pp. 290-291. Printed in "Poems. J. R.," pp. 23-24. Published in the American edition, pp. 7-8.

Note XXXIX. "Journal" (p. 181).—For the dates of this tour, see Biographical Notes for 1835, above. A reason for abandoning this poem, still stronger than any exhaustion of his descriptive powers, was that, before the author had been many weeks at home after this journey, he had discovered a new motive for poetry—his first love-affair (see the poems to Adèle, 1836, vol. ii. of these poems) ; and he had adopted a new model—Shelley (Præt. I. x. p. 336). This journal was written during the tour, as is implied in a remark in the prose postscript to the "Letter from Abroad" "I have poetry interminable, which you must not sleep over."

Note XL. "Canto I." stanza 13, (p. 188).—In lines 3 and 5 I have supplied words to fill out the metre, which, with the dactylic rhyme, needs 12 syllables. In stanza 17, lines 2, 4, and 6, alteration is less called for, as the scant metre is hardly noticed till you come to line 6. In stanzas 23 and 24, lines 2, 4, and 6 are all too short. This poem was never revised ; there is only the one copy.

Note XLI. "Canto I." stanza 18 (p. 192).—In the last line "gleams" is a correction by the author's father,—the only one of its kind,—for "looks."

Note XLII. "Canto I." stanzas 23-25 (pp. 194).—Geologists must remember that in 1835 diluvian theories were still in vogue.

Note XLIII. "Canto I." stanza 30 (p. 198).—The Dôle is 5505 feet above the sea. The MS. reads very indistinctly, "3300" or "3900," an obvious clerical error, as 3900 feet do not nearly reach the snow-level.

Note XLIV. "Canto I." stanza 42 (p. 205).—Mr. Ruskin's first published writing is a letter to Loudon's *Mag. of Natural History* (*March* 1834), entitled "Enquiries on the Causes of the Colour of the Water of the Rhine," in which he describes the colour-phenomena of the Rhone and Lake of Geneva, and asks for an explanation from the scientific people. He appears to have got none, as usual.

Note XLV. "Canto II." stanza 2 (p. 209).—The Môle is 6125 feet above the sea, and 4665 above Bonneville : the Brezon is 6142 feet above the sea, and 4682 above Bonneville.

Note XLVI. "Canto II." stanza 7 (p. 212).—In line 12, "boil" in the original is "came," which belongs to the next line. In stanza 9, line 9, the original reads "rocks around him ;" but to rhyme with "rebounding" and "resounding" the word wanted is "surrounding." In stanza II' line 9, "watch the night decay" is in the original "watch the night away;" the last word evidently belongs to line 7.

Note XLVII. "Letter from Abroad," *Paris* (p. 224).— The "last midsummer" (1834) the two boys had spent together at Herne Hill.

Note XLVIII. "Letter," *St. Bernard* (p. 226).—"In the Annual Continental" refers to Prout's "Continental Annual." The visit to Chamouni is ignored in this Letter.

Note XLIX. "Letter," *Schaffhausen* (p. 227).—"Aosta" was the Augusta Prætoria Salassiorum of the Romans,—the Salassi being the old Gaulish inhabitants of the valley of the Duria (Doire).

Note L. "Letter," *Rigi* (p. 230).—"Granson" (Grandson), on the Lake of Neuchâtel, was the scene of the decisive victory of the Swiss over Charles the Bold, March 3, 1476; interesting to the author from the description in Sir W· Scott's "Anne of Geierstein" (chap. xxxii.). "Gessler" in the original is "Gesner," obviously a slip of the pen.

Note LI. "Letter," *Hospice of Grimsel* (p. 231).— "By Severn's stream." R. Fall would have returned to school by the 25th of August, according to the time of the old-fashioned holidays. Dr. Dale, his schoolmaster, is not the Mr. Dale to whom the author went to school in 1834, and lectures in 1836.

Note LII. "Letter," *Hospice of Grimsel* (p. 232).—"St. Gothard—mineralogy." De Saussure, already, as afterward, the author's "master in geology" (Præt. I. vii. p. 206; Modern Painters, vol. iv. p. 175 *note*), describes the St. Gothard minerals and rock structure with care (M. P., vol. iv. p. 301, and Appendix 2); regarding as mineralogical phenomena the contortion and brecciation which others regard as geological, and trying to account for them by aqueous crystallisation ; as if the agatescent minerals contained within the rock-masses were epitomes or microcosms of the whole mountain-chain.

Note LIII. "Letter," *Hospice of Grimsel* (p. 233) "The vapours came with constant crowd." In "Modern Painters," vol. I. ii. 3, 4, § 31–34 (pp. 258–260), a famous passage begins " Stand upon the peak of an isolated mountain at daybreak," and goes on to describe an Alpine morning,—storm,—sunset,—moonlight,—and sunrise : asking " Has Claude given this ?" and, in notes, introducing various works of Turner as illustrating the sky effects of nature. The passage is quoted in " Frondes Agrestes," § 25, where in a note the author remarks," I have seen such a storm on the Rigi." In this letter we get the actual occasion, in the middle of *August* 1835; and find that the "Modern Painters" passage is a reminiscence of matter of fact. Beginning it with § 32, and keeping § 31 for the conclusion, we can compare it with this passage in the "Letter," and find, in both, the gathering storm,—the sweeping apart of the clouds by sudden wind,— the lurid sunset and thunderstorm,—gradually clearing up to moonlight ; the purple dawn and sunrise on snow-peaks ; and fine morning with mist in the valleys.

Note LIV. " Venice" (p. 236) —Intended for the Journal, and possibly written at Venice, *Oct.* 6–17, 1835, or at any rate soon after.

Note LV. "Salzburg" (p. 238).—The author visited Salzburg for the first time in *Oct.* 1835. This piece was published in "Friendship's Offering," 1835, pp. 37–38, with an engraving by E. Goodall of "Saltzburg" (*sic*) from a drawing by W. Purser. It was omitted in "Poems. J. R," and is the first piece in the American edition (pp. 1–3). In the note in both editions, "St. Rupert" reads "St. Hubert" twice over, —wrongly, for it was Hruadprecht or Rupert, Bishop of Worms, who, at the close of the seventh century, established the monastic colony of Salzburg among the ruins of the Roman city of Juvava. Towards the middle of the eighth century the monk Virgilius from Ireland built a church at Salzburg, dedicated it to St. Rupert, and became first Archbishop of Salzburg. Many of the apostles of Germany, both before and after Rupert, were English, like Boniface, or Scots from Ireland or Iona, like Columban and Gall; but I confess I have not been able to assure myself of Rupert's Scottish origin; while St. Hubert was a native of Aquitaine.

Note LVI. "The Avalanche" (p. 240).—Printed in "Poems. J. R.," pp. 5–7.

Note LVII. "The Emigration of the Sprites" (p. 243).— Printed in "Poems. J. R.," pp. 13–19. The original occurs with "The Avalanche" and "The Invasion of the Alps" in Note-book No. VIII.; they are dated from their position in section (*c.*) (see Preliminary Note). Stanzas VII. and VIII. refer to "The Brownie of Bodsbeck," a story by the author's friend James Hogg, the Ettrick Shepherd.

Note LVIII. "Conversation" (p. 251).—"Miss R.,"—Mary Richardson, the author's cousin and adopted sister (Præt. I. iv. p. 111). "Mary" was Mary Stone, cook at Herne Hill,

1827-36. "I have never seen a fillet of veal rightly roasted, nor a Yorkshire pudding rightly basted, since Mary Stone left us to be married in 1836." "Lucy,"—"Our perennial parlour maid, Lucy Tovey, came to us in 1829, remaining with us till 1875" (Præt. II. vi. p. 191). Mr. Ruskin says (Præt. I. vii. p. 237), "I can scarcely account to myself, on any of the ordinary principles of resignation, for the undimmed tranquillity of pleasure with which, after these infinite excitements in foreign lands, my father would return to his desk opposite the brick wall of the brewery, and I to my niche behind the drawing-room chimney-piece. But to both of us, the steady occupations, the beloved samenesses, and the sacred customs of home were more precious than all the fervours of wonder in things new to us, or delight in scenes of incomparable beauty."

END OF VOL. I.

PRINTED BY BALLANTYNE, HANSON AND CO.
EDINBURGH AND LONDON.

Lightning Source UK Ltd.
Milton Keynes UK
UKOW06f1832100816

280419UK00009B/157/P

9 781332 840182